MW00770965

THE SECOND CRYPTO REVOLUTION

BUILD GENERATIONAL WEALTH WITH RICHARD HEART'S CRYPTO ECOSYSTEM

Jones Mablood

TABLE OF CONTENTS

INTRODUCTION

I heard about cryptocurrencies in Q1 2017 for the first time. The posts of a celebrity active in the business segment I used to study started to be pinned by him on my Facebook wall. He mainly wrote about two things: moving to Cambodia, where I was just about to start another job in tourism, and about a mysterious Bitcoin.

After a few weeks of reading his posts about Bitcoin's price movements ranging from $1,000 to $3,000, I set up an account on BitBay (now Zonda) – one of the cryptocurrency exchanges that is used as a trading market . As an experiment, I made a few, maybe over a dozen, cryptocurrency exchange trades. I could not get enough of trading some digital bells and whistles sometimes earning profit and sometimes losing money. In the meantime during my leisure when I did not have to work and was not preoccupied with my tropical Cambodian life, I would read and watch everything I could get my hands on concerning cryptocurrencies.

A while later I bought several cryptocurrencies and watched in disbelief as they all rose in value at a ferocious pace . I bought one of them for $200, only to sell it for $350 in just over a month, making a 75% profit on my investment. I felt like a genius not knowing that the cryptocurrency bull market had just started and if I had waited a few more months, I could have sold the same cryptocurrency for almost $1500!

For the rest of 2017, I made over a dozen more trades and became more and more convinced that I knew what I was doing. From today's perspective, my activity at that time looked like random button-pushing. As a result, I was the proud owner of over a dozen different cryptocurrencies and the value of my initial investment rose more than a dozen times.

However, these were only paper profits . In January 2018, the bear market started and due to my bone-deep stubbornness I sold nothing and watched in horror as my unrealized gains melted like snow in the first rays of the spring sun. Before I knew it, the value of my cryptocurrency portfolio was more or less at the same level from which I had started and the dreams of financial independence seemed to have become more distant again.

However, I have not stopped believing in the potential of cryptocurrencies and that they could one day transform my already fascinating life. It was probably for this reason that I pumped the entire handsome commission I received for giving a helping hand to close a certain deal in Burma (also known as Myanmar) into cryptocurrencies only to watch my investment just dwindle. It turned out that a 50% decline of the market capitalization was no bargain and the prices of all cryptocurrencies still had a long and painful way to go down.

Understanding well the sentential of Socrates: I only know one thing, and that is I know nothing, I discontinued speculating and went back to educating myself about cryptocurrencies.

On the onset of 2019, a good friend of mine - Konrad, drew my attention to the figure of Richard Heart and his first cryptocurrency, HEX. Initially, I ignored the topic because I could not help the feeling that this would be another get-rich-quick scheme in which I invested in 2017 and I would lose money again. However, the unexpected upheavals at work, made me take a closer look at the topic and after a few weeks I decided to convert almost all my cryptocurrencies into HEX. As it turned out later, it was one of the best decisions of my life.

***

To fully appreciate the rest of this story, it would be helpful if you get to know me a little better. My writing career started at the age of 16 with the publication of my first article for which I got paid . Over the next few years I wrote about everything from modern technology to travel and politics. The latter topic allowed me, a teenage diaper boy, to accompany the Polish President and Prime Minister during their trips on government plane to the USA, Israel and to NATO and European Union summits in Brussels.

After graduating from university with a degree in political science, I ignored an offer to take a job as a terrorist threat analyst at the Ministry of Defense (MoD), I gave up low-paying journalism and decided to see if the grass was greener in Ireland.

I quickly found a job in the business support department of a major consulting firm. I was earning good money which at that time in Poland you could only dream about. I rented a nice apartment, bought a car, a fancy TV and a PlayStation 3. I planned to buy a house with a mortgage loan and raise a family. Then it came – a depression caused by the terrible weather, corporate boredom and daily routine. I took my MA degree in broadly understood International Relations at the Dublin's Trinity College, but it did not make me feel any better. I decided to return to writing because it seemed to give me the greatest satisfaction.

However, in order to write, you have to have a topic to write about. A two-week getaway to Iran just before the presidential elections and the Green Movement in 2009, a 3-week road trip from New York to Los Angeles and, above all, a holiday in Thailand changed my life. I bought a one way ticket to the Southeast Asia and decided to become a famous foreign correspondent and writer. In the case of failure, Plan B was to attain English language teaching qualifications, to become a teacher and write after hours. It quickly became apparent that writing was a fun hobby, but as before, I was not able to earn enough from writing to support myself at a reasonable level. So I decided to pursue Plan B, which was followed by other plans .

Since my departure from Europe, I have lived in Burma, Thailand and Cambodia. I have travelled extensively in the Far East, from South Korea to East Timor. I spent a lot of time in the Latin America, from Colombia to Brazil. I worked as a lecturer at a university, as a manager of various departments in several travel companies and as a sales and marketing director in a luxury hotel owned by a well-known multinational corporation.

The COVID-19 pandemic killed global tourism and almost put an end to my crazy tropical life. I had just signed an employment contract for a new hotel management position, this time in Riyadh, when Saudi Arabia stopped issuing new visas and closed its borders. Shortly after, my would-be boss called me and told that, unfortunately, he had to withdraw his job offer.

However, this did not change the fact that I swapped tropical Cambodia for a desert climate anyway. Only not in the Middle East, but in Mexico where after a few months of lockdowns decision-makers decided that they cannot afford to continue this farce and almost fully opened up the country to tourism. I couldn't help thinking that if I was going to be able to find any reasonable employment anywhere under the prevailing circumstances it would be there....

And so we return to cryptocurrencies. My investment in HEX began to grow up like crazy and I gradually started to grasp that I might not need a job at all, neither in Mexico nor anywhere else. The smell and a breath of financial independence gave me a boost again and made me buy a Thailand Elite visa, allowing me a 5-year legal stay in the country. Consequently I packed my bag and moved again down under .

However, the joy of living in one of my favorite countries in the world did not last long because a few months later the government threatening with Covid pandemic closed down gyms, swimming pools, parks, restaurants, bars and shopping malls. Life in Bangkok became unbearable. The ever-increasing price of HEX made me decide to invest in Richard Heart's next project, PulseChain. My newly achieved financial independence enabled me to travel for several months to Brazil, Peru, Paraguay, Argentina, Canada, and the Dominican Republic.

On the way back to Bangkok I stopped in London, where HEX's second birthday had just been celebrated. I met Richard Heart in person there, which was the main reason for my European stop over before returning home. Shaking hands with the man who allowed me to completely opt out of further participation in the rat race led me to investment in his latest project, PulseX, a few weeks later.

I am spending 2022 enjoying life in Thailand, writing this book and waiting for the release of PulseChain and PulseX which should take the size of my financial independence to the levels I never even thought of just a few years ago. As my story shows, life is full of opportunities you never even dreamt of. While the invention of Bitcoin was the First Crypto revolution, the second one has just now begun.

ABOUT THE BOOK

It is impossible to fully grasp the potential of cryptocurrencies without prior understanding what money actually is, where it came from and how it evolved. In Chapter One, therefore, I will provide you with a brief definition of money and tell you something about its history from antiquity to modern times. In Chapter Two, I will provide you with a brief historical outline of banks, from keeping cash in temples in antiquity to the 2007/2008 financial crunch. But do not worry, historical outline is presented in a very concise manner!

In Chapter Three we will get to the heart of the matter. I explain what cryptocurrencies really are and where they come from. I'll give you a brief historical context of them and talk about their advantages and disadvantages. In this chapter, you will also learn more about Bitcoin and Ethereum – the two largest cryptocurrencies. I conclude with a thesis that the cryptocurrency system is fundamentally corrupt, mentioning fraud, hacking and other hoaxes associated with it.

Chapter Four, will introduce you to three of the most influential people in the cryptocurrency industry. These are, of course, the Bitcoin and Ethereum founders: Satoshi Nakamoto and Vitalik Buterin as well as Richard Heart – the founder of a new cryptocurrency ecosystem, addressing most (if not all) of the problems currently faced by the crypto industry. At this point the first part of the book, The First Crypto Revolution , ends and the second part begins.

Chapters Five, Six and Seven will introduce you consistently to the first products that are part of the Richard Heart ecosystem:

- HEX – The First Blockchain Certificate of Deposit,
- PulseChain – a cheaper, faster and energy-efficient alternative to Ethereum,
- PulseX – the most liquid exchange on PulseChain.

Chapter Eight, moves towards practice and teaches you how to make money on the Second Crypto Revolution in the years to come. It will be about setting up and using an account on an exchange, required to start investing in cryptocurrencies, how to set up and operate a cryptocurrency wallet and how to invest in new revolutionary products in the crypto industry.

Chapter Nine focuses on security. You'll learn from it about crypto exchanges, wallets, scammers, hackers, laptops and phones as well as taking care of yourself in the real world. After all, no investment is worth your health or your life!

If, like me, you decide to join the Second Crypto Revolution, there is a very good chance that you will become financially successful in ways you never even dreamt of. It can, however, make the tax office of the country you live in to take a quick interest in your money. If you don't live in a place where the tax system is crypto-investor friendly, I'll give you some tips on what you can do about it in Chapter Ten.

The Second Crypto Revolution is a book written primarily for the 99% of people in the world without any experience with cryptocurrencies yet. It will also benefit those who already have experience with cryptocurrencies, but so far have not made as much money from them as they expected. Perhaps you bought Bitcoin for $69,000 or Ethereum for $4,800 and have been sitting on a paper loss for months. Perhaps you have lost a lot of money in the Celsius system, Luna or on FTX. If so, this book is for you too.

I tried to use the most straightforward language I could, for instance when comparing the technology behind cryptocurrencies to a spreadsheet, and the special password for a crypto wallet to the PIN required for your ATM card. I have simplified many concepts as much as possible which can have made some of them not 100% accurate and my understanding of them may look wrong at first glance. This is deliberate because the crypto industry is very technical, full of jargon and not very user-friendly. If your goal is to become a rentier thanks to cryptocurrencies, do you really need to know and understand all the subtleties regarding, for instance, the various consensus mechanisms on the Blockchain right from the start?

As a bonus, I am adding an online list of websites worth watching for current and future cryptocurrency investors as well as information on where to find me and how to contact me.

Without further delay, let's get down to business. Financial independence is within your reach!

PART I

THE FIRST CRYPTO REVOLUTION

CHAPTER 1
DEFINITION AND HISTORY OF MONEY

An ancient Lydia coin – 6th century BC.

Our made up imaginary internet money is better than the governments' made up imaginary internet money. Both of them are only backed by the shared fiction of the humans believing that they have value

Richard Heart in the documentary The Highest of Stakes

Coins, banknotes, credit cards, lines of figures visible in your bank account... have you ever wondered what money really is? It is nothing more than a legal tender with a certain value attached that supports the exchange of goods and services, informs about product prices and provides a means of wealth accumulation. Money is a unit of account that is a socially accepted standard by which things are valued and by which payments are made. Money and currency according to some definitions are not identical concepts. Money is an intangible concept, while currency is a physical tender that merely expresses the money concept. Money has undergone a huge evolution: from bullion- or furs-based barter , through the first coins, to banknotes and credit cards. Let us take a closer look at the history of money and banking, from antiquity to modern times.

FROM BARTER TO CURRENCY

In Antiquity, before the first coins were developed , easily tradable objects such as animal skins, salt or weapons became currency and served as a medium of exchange. Barter became more and more widespread throughout the world. The invention of money took place even before the beginning of written history but we are unable to ascertain in which country it originated. This is due to the lack of records and the different paces of development of ancient civilizations.

The oldest types of money are money of account (debits and credits on ledgers) and barter money (items that were used for barter). The earliest money of account is the Ishango Bone found near one of the sources of the Nile in the Democratic Republic of Congo, which was probably used to count and record the numerical system. Accounting records dating back more than 7,000 years ago have also been found in Mesopotamia. These documents show lists of expenses and a goods received and sold.

Money of exchange originated well before coins were invented. In ancient Egypt, Babylon, India and China, clay tokens and other materials were found that acted as evidence of claims to commodities placed in warehouses and could be exchanged as an object of trade. Metals (common and precious) were used in barter and monetary systems, laying the foundations for monetary systems. In ancient Rome, rough bronze (aes rude) was used for barter exchange, which was the form of a bronze weight.

The first coins have been discovered within the territory of China. A group of archaeologists from Zhengzhou State University discovered a mint located in Guanzhuang, Henan Province, where spade coins were minted. These were probably the first standardized metal coins and are considered to be the first coins created by the mankind.

During the same era in ancient Greece, the first official currency was minted in the

6th century BC. This was the Lydian stater minted by order of the Lydian king – Alyattes (600 BC). The world's first currency was minted from electrum, a mixture of silver and gold, and had images that were treated as denominations. The existence of the currency became the catalyst for Lydia development , which was recorded in history as one of the richest empires in Asia Minor. It was the name of the Lydian king Croesus, who accumulated a lot of wealth and minted the first gold coin, that became synonymous with rich man. Hence the origin of the often-used phrase: As rich as Croesus. Ancient Sparta minted iron coins to discourage citizens from trading abroad. Other countries minted coins of gold and silver.

Despite the fact that the first coins were minted in Lydia and Greece, it is the Phoenicians who are responsible for the spread of money-based trade. They were an ancient merchant people living in the Mediterranean countries. The Phoenicians spread money, which became the foundation of their wealth. Thanks to the Phoenicians' well-developed trade network, money spread across the globe. Money acquired a new function, in addition to being a means of payment it also became a symbol of power.

In the 13th century, gold coins started to be minted again in Europe. Frederick II is credited with the reintroduction of gold coins during the Crusades. In the 14th century, Europe switched from silver to gold, which was used as a means of payment. Vienna made this change in 1328. In the 17th century, plate money was produced in Sweden from large slabs of copper which were stamped with their value, as there was a shortage of precious metals.

How did coins come to be introduced in Europe to replace primary money? Merchants of the time realized that commodities such as furs could be hardly divided and that grain varied in value depending on the season. As a result, this led to the use of metals as a means of payment which initiated the development of money. Initially, people paid with metal bars or lumps of bullion but they were difficult to transport. So they started to divide them into balls, which were later signed with the seals of the rulers, giving rise to coins. Originally coins were minted from various metal alloys, and over time they were minted from gold and silver alloy only.

The Middle Ages are referred to as the Dark Ages but in terms of the monetary expansion rate it is closer to the Enlightenment. Coin minting techniques were excelled, which contributed to trade development. The right to produce money belonged to the ruler at the time and only occasionally could it be delegated to the clergy.

In the Middle Ages, the so-called money merchants emerged to deal with currency exchange. At that time, they faced problems such as counterfeiting of coins, manipulation of the bullion content and the large number of coin makers. In the Middle Ages, the first bankers started to take the lead, offering the customers a service involving depositing money at their place and withdrawing it elsewhere on the basis of a depository receipt, which became the prototype of banks. The first bank was established in 1156 in Venice, which was a catalyst for the development of the financial and credit system of medieval Europe.

The spread of money became the subject of philosophical reflection. St. Thomas Aquinas accepted trading and lending to Christians on the condition that the customer received a fair return. Nicolaus Copernicus, on the other hand, in his Monetae cudendae ratio (English Treatise On the Minting of Coin), created the law of debasement of coinage[1].

The Chinese replaced coins with paper money around 10th century and it did not become common in Europe until the 17th century. Banknotes followed the issuing of depository receipts by goldsmiths and bankers, which they used for settlement because they were more convenient than coins. This started the process that led to the spread of notes and the acceptance of the idea by government authorities. Banks also began to use paper notes which were more convenient than coins for customers or borrowers. Banknotes could be exchanged for silver or gold coins at any time. Money was becoming more and more popular and goods and services could be bought with it. At that time the banks were responsible for issuing currency.

The first paper currency of the European governments was issued by their colonial governments in the North America. The reason for its issue was the lack of cash in the colonies, so the governments there issued IOUs[2], which were exchangeable for currency. In 1685, soldiers were provided with playing cards with the denomination and signature of the governor to use as cash instead of coins from France.

BANKNOTES IN EUROPE

The forerunner of the banknotes implementation in Europe is Sweden. The Stockholms Banco issued paper money for the first time in Europe. They replaced the copper plates that had been used as a means of payment. Banks issued banknotes at the time and put them into circulation, just as national governments do today. Furthermore, they were responsible for issuing banknotes in England until 1694, while in Scotland the last time a bank issued banknotes was in 1850. In the United States, on the other hand, this practice continued throughout the 19th century. More than 5000 different types of banknotes were issued in the USA. They were printed by many American banks. Only banknotes issued by the largest banks with the best creditworthiness were accepted, while those issued by smaller institutions were in local circulation . Banknotes were, at the time, a form of representative money that could be exchanged for gold or silver at a bank. A paradox occurred when banks issued banknotes in the quantities exceeding their deposited gold and silver reserves . This could have led to the bankruptcy of numerous financial institutions.

In India, the earliest paper money was issued by the Bank of Hindustan (1770-1832), the General Bank of Bengal and Bihar (1773-1775) and the Bengal Bank (1784-1791). Over time, however, governments became responsible for issuing banknotes. After 1694, the Bank of England was given the exclusive right to issue banknotes. In the United States, the Federal Reserve Bank was granted similar powers after its foundation in 1913.

Until 1971, currency in the USA was a form of representative money that was partly backed by gold or silver bullions and were convertible into them. It was not until

President Richard Nixon introduced a rule stating that the US dollar would not be convertible into gold. The rule introduced by Nixon led to the US dollar losing its backing in gold, becoming a paper whose value is determined by virtue of social agreement and the government can print as much as it wants, which is the direct cause of inflation.

At the end of the 20th century, credit and debit cards began to take the lead in making payments worldwide. The first credit card in the USA was a card issued by the Bank of America called BankAmericard with a revolving credit facility and a limit of $300. It became the prototype for the later Visa payment system. Eight years later, the first version of the Mastercard system appeared in the market.

In Europe, the first credit card was the one issued by the Barclays bank in Great Britain in 1966. Three years later, IBM developed the magnetic stripe, which was implemented in credit cards, becoming the standard adopted around the globe. It is worth knowing that previously, machines would take a credit card imprint and send it to a processing center where a clerk would enter the credit card account data into a computer system. The magnetic stripe reduced the credit card payment process to approximately one minute.

SUMMARY

- Money carries the value people assign to it.
- Money enables indirect trade in goods and services, communicates the price of goods and provides a mean for wealth accumulation.
- Before the invention of money, people acquired and exchanged goods through barter.
- The world's oldest known mint house was in Guanzhuang in Henan province, China, where spade coins began to be minted

around 640 BC, probably as the first standardized metal coin.

- In the same era, the first official currency was minted in ancient Greece in the 6th century BC.

- The first banknote was issued in China around the 10th century. The banknotes did not become widespread in Europe until 17th century.

- The first paper currency of the European governments was issued by their colonial governments in North America.

- The forerunner of the banknotes implementation in Europe is Sweden. Stockholms Banco issued the first paper money in Europe.

- Until 1971, currency in the USA was a form of representative money that was partly backed by gold or silver bullions and convertible into them. It was not until President Richard Nixon introduced a rule stating that the US dollar would not be convertible into gold, making its value governed by social agreement.

- At the end of 20th century, credit and debit cards started to take the lead in the payment industry worldwide.
- The first credit card in the USA was a card issued by Bank of America called the BankAmericard with a revolving credit facility and a limit of $300.
- In Europe, the first credit card was the one issued by the Barclays Bank in Great Britain in 1966.

---

[1] It is a law stating that if there are two types of money at the same time, legally equivalent, but one of them is perceived to be better, this better money will be collected and the worse money will mainly remain in circulation. This law expresses the buzzword that bad money drives out good money.

[2] It is a phonetic abbreviation for I owe you (IOU) – a document that acknowledges the existence of a debt. It is an obligation seen as an informal social agreement.

CHAPTER 2
A BRIEF HISTORY OUTLINE OF BANKING

The Old Town Hall in Amsterdam where the Bank of Amsterdam was founded in 1609, painting by Pieter Saenredam.

If the American people ever allow private banks to control the issue of their currency, first by inflation, then by deflation, the banks... will deprive the people of all property until their children wake up homeless on the continent their Fathers conquered.... The issuing power should be taken from the banks and restored to the people, to whom it properly belongs.

Thomas Jefferson (the third President of the United States) in the debate on the transformation of the Banking Act (1809)

It was in ancient Babylon where debt money was traded which was concentrated in the temples and generated skyrocketing profits for the priests[3]. During the Babylonian captivity in 6th century BC Jews set up their own banks. We date the beginning of the banking era in Europe to the 4th century BC, when Isocrates, in his work Trapesitica, described the case of the defense of the favored Satyrus, the King of the Bosporan Kingdom, whose entrusted money had been embezzled by an Athenian banker, a former slave, Pasion. The charged initially pleaded guilty but later covered up traces of the transaction and recanted his testimony. Information about accounting entries and deposit trading can already be found in the fiery speeches of one of the ancient Greece's most famous speakers, Demosthenes. Researchers claim that the banking collapses in Greece were linked to the crises of 377-376 and 371 BC. An important fact in the history of banking was the establishment of a state bank by the Egyptian Ptolemies (3rd - 1st century BC), whose services were also aimed at businessmen, artisans and minor banks.

In Antiquity, people kept money in temples because priests enjoyed a high degree of public trust. Over time, priests also began to lend money. Records from ancient Greece, Rome and Egypt attest to it. The ancient Romans moved banking out of the temples into separate buildings, providing usury services to the public in return for a profit charged on the amount borrowed. Julius Caesar, in one of his edicts, allowed land to be forfeited in case of a loan default .

In ancient Rome, banking associations, the so-called societas argentariae, were introduced and the bankers were called mensarii (from *mensa* – counting room, counter). They formed a guild to protect their interests. They were familiar with a concept such as the consumer loan (*mutuum*) which allowed banks to trade in deposited funds and pay interest to depositors. The Romans also distinguished between a loan for the temporary use of a thing (*commodatum*) and a deposit. Unfortunately, Rome's well-functioning financial system collapsed due to inflationary monetary policy and historical events such as the expansion of Christianity, the migration of peoples and the onslaught of the Germans.

The collapse of the Roman empire led to the destruction of the banking services, which were revived during the Crusades. In turn, papal bankers appeared on the scene, delivering various banking services. In the Middle Ages, the charging of interest was considered immoral and such practices were therefore prohibited. The Church opposed usury as early as 325 A.D., as stated by Pope Leo I at the Council of Nicaea. The Church's position on this issue was followed by Charlemagne who banned lay people from engaging in usury in 789 A.D.

Italy played a pivotal role in the history of banking. As early as 1157, the first bank, named Monte, was established, and shortly afterwards a second bank, Banco di Giro, was set up. The name bank comes from the Italian word banco, meaning a bench where money transactions took place. Banking services in Italy were delivered by the Acciaiuoli, Bonacorsi and Salimberi families.

There were frequent bankruptcies at the time which were due to accepting deposits based on the fractional reserve and the lending activities[4]. The Medici Bank in the 15th century was involved in accepting deposits called depositi discrezione. These were loans from depositors to the bank with which the bank granted credit, providing interest to the creditors. As a result, the Medici bank collapsed as they lost liquidity due to the loss of a significant portion of bank reserves.

The bank bankruptcies on a mass scale necessitated the enactment of a law in Barcelona, which stipulated that the name of a banker who went bankrupt was to be announced in the Catalan markets and the bankrupt banker was supposed to live eating only bread and drinking only water until he has repaid total debt. Subsequently, the death penalty for fraud was introduced for bankers. This happened to Francesco Castello, among others, in 1360. In response to the financial crunch, the Barcelona authorities set up a government-owned Municipal Bank.

In Germany, a bank was established in Hamburg in 1189. The Bank of Nuremberg was also established in 15th century to finance the activities of Emperor Maximilian. The Fugger family members became the bankers of Charles V, obtaining in exchange for loans, huge pledges in the form of mines and steelworks and enforcing the payment of tax arrears from creditors. The policies pursued by the rulers also led to bank failures. In 1575, Philip II caused the bankruptcy of the banks of Italy by issuing a debt decree, and due to a third bankruptcy of the King of Spain the Fuggers family lost 3.25 million ducats.

During the Renaissance period, banking operations became common. In 1609, the Bank of Amsterdam was established and for the first time in history it guaranteed to keep 100% reserves for demand deposits. The bank followed that principle for 170 years and, consequently, though it did not generate high income, but it survived all crises.

From the 16th century onwards, goldsmiths in England were involved in lending, currency exchange or bullion trading. Prior to this, it was the scribes who held deposits for lending. The merchants deposited gold with London goldsmiths, who had private vaults and charged service fees. For each deposit, goldsmiths issued receipts confirming the quantity and purity of the metal. The receipts were not transferable (i.e. could not be assigned to another person) and, over time, goldsmiths took on the role of scribes, making loans on behalf of the depositor. English goldsmiths delivered their banking services by issuing bills of exchange for deposited money, which represented a loan to the goldsmith. As bills of exchange were payable on demand and loans to the goldsmith's customers were repayable over a longer period, this was an early form of fractional reserve banking. Bills of exchange became a convenient form of money with a guarantee of payment from the goldsmith.

In 1694, the Bank of England was established in the British isles, which suspended its banking operations in 1797 following a scandal caused by the speculations of colonial companies. In 1656 the Bank of Sweden was established which was later nationalized and is considered the first modern state bank. This bank started to issue depository receipts (notes) for an amount higher than the value of the deposit, which had impact on the underlying bullion money and created artificial demand.

In 18th century France, John Law, the financier, became the author of a new banking system that involved issuing too many banknotes and creating a speculative bubble. The bubble burst in 1720 and resulted in the collapse of the East India Company. The 1880s saw inflation and financial chaos, which became one of the causes of the Great French Revolution.

Adam Smith introduced the theory of the invisible hand, creating free market economy systems (1776). This had the effect of reducing state interference in the banking sector and in the economy. The ideas of the free market and capitalism perfectly established themselves in the USA. Indeed, in the United States, national banks were established to secure banknotes with the purchase of securities, which helped to ooze out the activities of state banks. In 1904, corporate banks were outlawed in the state of Texas.

In the 19th century, the Rothschilds were regarded to be the pioneers of the banking sector, lending to the Bank of England and buying government bonds in the stock exchanges . Their wealth was believed to be the largest in modern history. Nathan Mayer Rothschild not only traded in financial instruments on the stock exchange, but later also started to trade in gold, which became the foundation of his business. From 1811 onwards, he started to finance the English army, also during the battles fought against Napoleon.

The Rothschilds also supported the railway systems, contributing their capital to fund such projects as the Suez Canal. They became the owners of numerous companies: Alliance Assurance (1824; now Royal & SunAlliance), Chemin de Fer du Nord (1845), Rio Tinto Group (1873), Société Le Nickel (1880; now Eramet) and Imétal (1962; now Imerys). The Rothschilds financed many ventures, including Cecil Rhodes' expeditions to Africa and the establishment of the Rhodesia colony.

During the Napoleonic Wars, France became an international financial center with a national bank and a whole range of private banks. Rothschild founded the De Rothschild Frères bank in 1812. An interesting fact about the Rothschild bank is that it financed France's wars and its colonial expansion.

Merchant banks such as Goldman Sachs, Kuhn, Loeb & Co. and J.P. Morgan & Co. played a large role in the history of banking.

Their main source of profit included commissions on the sale of foreign bonds from Europe. At the time, banks were required to disclose capital reserves, so family-owned merchant banks existed for years and enjoyed a good reputation.

A breakthrough event in the history of banking was the establishment of the Federal Reserve Bank (FED) in 1913. This was the beginning of a new era that limited the activities and economic influence of commercial banks.

The United States became a global lender during the World War I. Due to 1929 stock-market crash, the global economy was destroyed. As many as 9,000 companies went bankrupt at that time. An important law introduced by the US government was the Glass-Steagall Act. According to the Act, commercial banks were banned to speculate on consumer deposits.

Further changes occurred during World War II. The FED and banks had to perform huge financial transactions worth billions of dollars, which led to the establishment of companies with huge lending demand and mergers of the banks to satisfy market demand. There was a globalization of banks that operated on a global scale. Domestic banks in the USA then gained consumer confidence with deposit insurance and the expansion of mortgage lending, which increased access to lending facilities and interest in them.

A milestone in the global banking development was the launch of online banking services. This took place at the turn of the 20th century, with the origins dating back to as early as 1980s. The growing popularity of smartphones accelerated the expansion of mobile banking services and today almost everyone makes transfers through an online banking system. A 2021 J.D. Power's study shows that as many as 41% of respondents use digital banking exclusively.

The 2007/2008 banking crisis led to the collapse of the high-risk mortgage market in the USA and had serious repercussions on a worldwide basis. The cause of the crisis was the granting of mortgages to people with insufficient financial capacity and such loans were used as collaterals for structured bonds, which were sold for investment and speculative purposes. The insolvency of bank customers led to a shortage of cash in the lending market and instability and also to the collapse of Lehman Brothers. The events back in those days showed that banks had lost track of reality, offering products that were beyond comprehension of their personnel and extending loans to people who could not afford them. The 2007/2008 financial crunch severely undermined confidence in banks and may have been the beginning of the end of the banking era as we know it.

SUMMARY

- In Antiquity, people kept money in temples, because priests enjoyed a high degree of public trust.

- The beginning of the banking era in Europe dates back to 4th century BC.

- During the Babylonian captivity in 6th BC Jews set up their own banks.

- Italy has played a key role in the history of banking. As early as in 1157, the first bank called Monte was established.

- The term bank is derived from the Italian word banco meaning a bench where money transactions took place.

- Adam Smith introduced the theory of the invisible hand, creating free market economy systems (1776).

- Merchant banks such as Goldman Sachs, Kuhn, Loeb & Co. and J.P. Morgan & Co. played a major role in the history of banking.

- A breakthrough event in banking history was the establishment of the Federal Reserve Bank (FED) back in 1913.

- The United States became a global lender during World War I.
- Due to 1929 stock-market crash, the global economy was destroyed.
- A milestone in the global banking development was the introduction of online banking services. This took place at the turn of the 20th century .
- The 2007/2008 banking crisis led to the collapse of the high-risk mortgage market in the USA and had serious repercussions on a worldwide basis.

---

3   Debt money is currency issued by a government that is not backed by any physical commodity such as gold or silver but by the government that issued it. The value of debt money is derived from the relationship between supply and demand and the stability of the issuing government rather than the value of the commodity backing it. Most modern currencies like the euro and the US dollar are a type of debt money.

4   Partial Reserves are one component of the banking system that involves investing funds from customer deposits while only a small portion of these deposits are held as cash and remain available for withdrawal. The fractional reserve system is a way for banks to

profit from their investments.

CHAPTER 3
INTRODUCTION TO CRYPTOCURRENCIES

This is a force that is not going to go away. The cryptocurrencies are not going to go away.
And at some point the people that you met that you thought were crazy loon birds are going to be in the one

percent. They are going to be the
people that own half of everything.
– Richard Heart in the documentary The Highest of Stakes

DEFINITION OF CRYPTOCURRENCIES AND BLOCKCHAIN TECHNOLOGY

Cryptocurrencies are virtual currencies that have no physical form and are based on a distributed accounting system. Distributed accounting allows online transactions to take place directly between users without intermediaries or third parties. This system provides faster transactions and greater security than traditional accounting.

Cryptocurrencies use cryptography to secure financial transactions which is where the name cryptocurrency comes from. Cryptography uses complex mathematical calculations to send encrypted messages between parties. Cryptography allows cryptocurrency transactions to be anonymous, better protected and without intermediaries such as governments, banks and other financial institutions.

Records of cryptocurrency transaction processes are stored on a Blockchain – a digital ledger, which is a type of database created to secure transaction records. All transactions are recorded in the so-called blocks. Bitcoin blocks are created on average every 10 minutes and saved one after the other, without an option to edit the transaction records in previous blocks, creating a kind of blockchain. Blockchain can be compared to a spreadsheet, storing the balances of all those who hold a particular cryptocurrency, which can transfer funds via user signatures.

Blockchain technology was first used when the Bitcoin cryptocurrency was introduced. A common mistake is to use the words Blockchain and Bitcoin interchangeably because they are in fact two different concepts. Bitcoin is the world's first cryptocurrency and Blockchain is the registration system that, among other things, allows transactions to be made through this cryptocurrency.

A distinguishing feature of cryptocurrencies is that they are not issued by a central authority. The decentralized control of cryptocurrencies makes it independent of government decisions or central bank influence.

BLOCKCHAIN FOR TECHNOPHOBES

Blockchain is a method of storing a list of entries that cannot be easily changed once they have been created. This includes the list itself. The whole works on concepts from cryptography, including digital signatures and hash functions.

In most cases, the Blockchain is managed by a peer-to-peer network. All peer participants in the network use a common protocol that determines how they should communicate with each other, how a new block is created and verified. Once data is registered in any block, it can no longer be changed. Change of a given block means that all blocks following must also be changed. Depending on the protocol, this will require the agreement of most or even all network participants.

Blockchains are inherently secure. Blockchain technology is used where proper record keeping is important. Its applications include medical records, identity management, food traceability and voting, among others.

WHERE DO CRYPTOCURRENCIES COME FROM?

Cryptocurrencies are created in different ways. One method of obtaining them is through Proof of Work (PoW), also known as the process of mining cryptocurrencies by miners. A miner is a person with a computer running software to mine cryptocurrencies.

The process is called mining because, like any other natural resource, in most cases only a limited amount of a given cryptocurrency exists. For example, there will only be 21 million Bitcoins in existence and to date a little over 19 million have been mined.

Mining traditional commodities (e.g. gold) requires investment in excavators, dredgers and other machinery. With cryptocurrencies, the miner invests in a powerful computer, also known as a miner, to solve complex mathematical problems. When these are solved, the system creates new coins and awards them to the miner who solved them.

Miners also use their computers to verify transactions and to counter fraud in the system. The more miners working online, the faster the transaction verification and the less opportunity for fraud. The miner is paid for verifying transactions which is a small percentage of the total value of the transaction. A miner can therefore make money in two ways: by mining cryptocurrencies and by validating the transactions.

The second method of acquiring cryptocurrencies is the so-called Proof of Stake (PoS) – an alternative mechanism for verifying transactions and creating new blocks on the Blockchain.

The owners of PoS cryptocurrencies offer their already owned coins as collateral to validate transactions. They become validators, i.e. the equivalent of miners from proof of work systems. The process of pledging coins is commonly known as staking. Validators are selected to verify transactions based on the number of staked coins in the system.

In order to become a validator, the owner of a specific cryptocurrency has to stake a certain number of coins. For example, Ethereum requires a minimum of 32 ETH to be staked. Validators, like miners, earn money by securing the Blockchain and verifying blocks with transactions.

THE HISTORY OF CRYPTOCURRENCIES DRIVEN BY THE NEED FOR INDEPENDENCE FROM THE CENTRAL CURRENCY SYSTEM

The forerunner of cryptocurrencies was David Chaum, an American cryptographer, who developed an anonymous, cryptographic electronic money called **ecash** in 1983. He implemented it in 1995, making it available as electronic payments system. It required software that enabled the withdrawal of notes from the bank. The software was also necessary to receive encryption keys that ensured the transaction security.

In 1996, the cryptocurrency system was described in How to Make a Mint: the Cryptography of Anonymous Electronic Cash, published by the National Security Agency. It was published on the MIT mailing list and later in The American Law Review (1997).

In 1998, Wei Dai, founder of the Crypto ++ cryptography library developed the B-money currency which he described in a publication as an anonymous, distributed, electronic cash system. The B-money system assumed that the currency could be transferred over a decentralized network and had the means to enforce contracts within the network without the use of a third party services. It was an attempt to create an anonymous and secure electronic transaction system that ultimately failed. Wai can be said to have laid the foundations for Bitcoin, whereas its founder, Satoshi

Nakamoto, himself referred to the B-money components in the Bitcoin Whitepaper – a document describing the foundations of the Bitcoin system published more than 10 years later.

At the same time, Nick Szabo developed another electronic currency system, Bit Gold, which should not be confused with a modern exchange with a similar name. It featured a proprietary system that was similar to the modern cryptocurrency mining process. Szabo wanted Bit Gold to reflect the properties of real gold without the need for intermediaries during transactions. Bit Gold was based on cryptography and was intended to function like a modern Blockchain but this project also went up in smoke. However, it became a huge inspiration for future developers who succeeded in bringing their cryptocurrencies to market.

In 2007-2008, there was a financial crunch that caused the so-called Great Recession. It led to a drop in housing prices, a drastic increase in unemployment and the bankruptcy of some 2.5 million companies in the USA. These events were one of the reasons for Bitcoin development.

In April 2011, Namecoin was developed as an attempt to set up a decentralized system that would make Internet censorship more difficult. This was soon followed by Litecoin in October 2011 which had the ambition to become a faster Bitcoin. With each consecutive year, more and more cryptocurrencies were created.

On 6 August 2014, the HM Treasury announced the commissioning of a study on cryptocurrencies and the role they could play in the British economy. The study was also to determine whether regulation was needed in this area. The final report was published in 2018 and HM Treasury carried out consultations concerning cryptocurrencies in January 2021.

In June 2021, El Salvador became a major center for cryptocurrencies by accepting Bitcoin as legal tender in the country. This happened after the Legislative Assembly passed a bill submitted by President Nayib Bukele with a vote count of 62-22. Cuba followed into the footsteps of El Salvador and adopted Resolution No. 215 in August 2021, which recognized cryptocurrencies such as Bitcoin and regulated their operation.

In September 2021, the Chinese government made all cryptocurrency transactions illegal. This was the culmination of the authorities' years-long fight against cryptocurrencies which was preceded by a ban on intermediaries and crypto-miners within China.

In turn, in the face of Russian invasion of Ukraine, President Volodymyr Zelensky signed a bill that legalized selected cryptocurrencies in Ukraine, making them legal tender in the country in March 2022. This decision was prompted by the fact that Ukraine has received more than $100 million in donations in the form of cryptocurrencies to help the country in its fight against the aggressor. In September last year, President Zelensky rejected a similar legislative proposal but in the face of war decided to join El Salvador in legalizing cryptocurrencies so as not to lose the donated funds denominated in cryptocurrencies.

ADVANTAGES OF CRYPTOCURRENCIES

The introduction of Bitcoin to the global markets has certainly revolutionized monetary transactions and the global financial system. Thirteen years since Bitcoin's debut, tens of thousands of new cryptocurrencies have been created, bringing many benefits to users around the world every day.

The first and fundamental benefit of cryptocurrencies is the emergence of a decentralized monetary system without the intermediation of banks and institutions and the supervision of transactions. The second benefit of some cryptocurrencies is often lower transaction fees than in traditional banking. **The last and by far the most important benefit of cryptocurrencies is the generation of profits.** Many people have made fortunes in this sector and the cryptocurrency markets were worth \$3 trillion by the end of 2021. By investing or speculating on cryptocurrencies, it is possible to make big money. The limited supply of countable digital currencies due to a top-down and limited number of units will lead to greater price stability in the future.

DISADVANTAGES OF CRYPTOCURRENCIES

Just as the banking system, the cryptocurrency system is full of flaws and risks. Firstly, let us take a closer look at the anonymity of transactions, which is only apparent, as every transaction leaves a digital footprint in the network that can be found by government agencies such as the FBI, CIA or NSA. This opens up an opportunity of tracking the transactions of ordinary citizens under the pretext of fighting crime, destroying the foundations of cryptocurrencies whose underlying foundations include anonymity and independence from central banks or institutions.

The disadvantage of cryptocurrencies has become their use by criminals who use Bitcoin, among others, for money laundering or illegal purchases of drugs, weapons or pornography involving minors. It should be noted that there has been a recent decline in crime involving cryptocurrencies from 0.62% to 0.15% of all transactions made in 2020 -2021. Hackers have also established themselves in the cryptocurrency industry to steal and extort money.

Another disadvantage of cryptocurrencies is that the industry is developing towards centralization because, despite the absence of banking supervision, only 10% of miners are responsible for more than 90% of the mining capacity in the case of Bitcoin. As a result, the cryptocurrency mining business is concentrated in the hands of large companies because it requires a huge amount of money. Energy consumption for mining activities is at least as high as that of entire countries!

CRYPTOCURRENCIES FOR TECHNOPHOBES

Cryptocurrency is a type of currency that uses digital files as money. Typically, the files are created using the same methods as cryptography (the science of hiding information). Digital signatures can be used to secure transactions and allow others to verify that transactions are genuine. The first cryptocurrencies were intended to be independent of government-issued currencies.

Cryptocurrencies use decentralized control, meaning that they are not controlled by one person or government. This differs from a centralized e-money and central banks. The control of each cryptocurrency works through a distributed ledger (a list of transactions shared by everyone), usually the Blockchain, which serves as a public database of financial transactions. Bitcoin, which was launched as open source software in 2009, is often referred to as the first decentralized cryptocurrency. Since then, more than 40,000 cryptocurrencies (sometimes called altcoins which is short for alternative coins) have been created.

BITCOIN – THE FORERUNNER OF CRYPTOCURRENCIES THAT REVOLUTIONIZED THE FINANCIAL WORLD

Bitcoin (₿) is a decentralized digital currency that is independent of central banks, administrators or financial institutions and can be transferred directly between users without any intermediaries. It is a modern way of protecting the value of money, similar to gold, and an innovative tool for making transactions all around the world.

Bitcoin can be exchanged for other currencies, products and services. It has no physical form and exists only virtually. It can be used to pay for certain services and products. Bitcoin is honored as a tender by large companies such as Microsoft and Expedia.

Bitcoin was invented by a software developer (or his team), Satoshi Nakamoto, in 2009. Bitcoin transactions are partially anonymous and verified by network nodes using cryptography and are kept in a chain of blocks in a public distributed ledger called Blockchain, which resembles a bank register.

Bitcoin has become an innovative digital currency using its own new transaction system, which has been created in opposition to the traditional financial system such as interbank transfers or Venmo and PayPal services.

Bitcoin operates in a distributed environment across the network and is not controlled by a single institution or bank, and anyone can become a user of this network.

An important aspect of Bitcoin is its resistance to inflation and manipulation by governments, corporations and other institutions.

Using Bitcoin is legal in most countries and the major method to earn profit is to invest and trade in Bitcoins , i.e. buying at a lower price and selling at a higher price.

The Bitcoin's value went up approximately 7 million times over a span of 12 years, from $0.01 in 2009 to almost $70,000 in 2021.

ETHER (ETH) – THE RUNNER-UP CRYPTOCURRENCY THAT IS GROWING IN STRENGTH

Ethereum is the runner-up Blockchain in terms of market capitalization. Market capitalization is the market value of a cryptocurrency listed at exchanges. Market capitalization is equal to the price of a cryptocurrency multiplied by the number of its units being traded.

Ethereum was created in 2013 by Vitalik Buterin, the software developer, and globally launched two years later. Ethereum was created as a decentralized computing platform for a wide range of applications. It is a decentralized Blockchain that has its own cryptocurrency, Ether. It is also a platform for many other crypto projects /assets, also known as tokens. The functionality of smart contracts enables the product development in such business segments as finance, gaming, advertising, Internet, identity management and supply chain management.

Ethereum also includes dollar-linked currencies: 1:1 called stablecoins and DeFi (Decentralized Finance) applications. These applications are operated under smart contracts, specifying the contracting terms between parties which, when fulfilled, are automatically executed. The contracting terms between the parties are written directly in the lines of code that control the execution and the transactions are traceable and irreversible.

Due to smart contracts, secure transactions can be made and contracts can entered into by and between anonymous parties without banking supervision or the legal system. One example of a smart contract is HEX which takes coins as a pledge for a user-specified period of time and gives them back with interest once the terms of the contract have been fulfilled.

Ether is the native token used in the Ethereum network. It is referred to as the ETH or simply Ethereum. Transactions involving Ether take place in a similar manner to that made with Bitcoin. Ether has another important function played in the Ethereum network because it is the fuel that guarantees the functioning of the entire system. ETH is referred to by many experts as the digital oil and Bitcoin as the digital gold.

Ethereum is often referred to as the World's Computer made up of many individual computers running Ethereum software. As with Bitcoin, keeping these computers running requires participants to invest in hardware and electricity. Many other crypto-assets are currently operated as Ethereum-based tokens.

According to Bloomberg News, Ethereum was the most frequently used Blockchain in 2020 and it had the highest number of followers of any cryptocurrency other than Bitcoin, according to the New York Times. Ethereum is currently implementing Ethereum 2.0, which includes but is not limited to a move to Proof of Stake (PoS) and enhanced transaction throughput. Ethereum has increased in value by approximately 30,000 times in six years, from $0.15 in 2015 to almost $5,000 in 2021.

BITCOIN AND ETHEREUM FOR TECHNOPHOBES

Bitcoin (₿) is a digital and global cryptocurrency in the monetary system. It enables people to send or receive money online, even to someone they do not know or trust. It is the first technology of its kind to allow digital goods to be transferred over the Internet without a need to get a third party involved. Money can be sent almost anonymously. Cryptography is at the heart of Bitcoin's security.

Ethereum is a system on the Web where people can make transactions. Ether is a type of money that uses the Ethereum system to make sure that each person gets the right amount in each transaction.

Ethereum was proposed in late 2013 by Vitalik Buterin, a cryptocurrency researcher and developer. Many people donated money to support the development of the system in one of the first initial coin offerings. The system entered the network on 30 July 2015 with 72 million coins. In 2016, Ethereum split into two separate versions, Ethereum and Ethereum Classic. In September 2022, it moved from Proof of Work to Proof of Stake as part of an update to the network known as Ethereum 2.0. Miners who lost their source of income from Ether mining and transactions verification disconnected from the main Ethereum chain and created Ethereum Proof of Work and Ethereum Fair. The future of both projects is unclear, but if Ethereum Classic is any indication then new versions of Ethereum will not be very popular and the most developed network will remain proper Ethereum based on proof of stake.

OTHER CRYPTOCURRENCIES

Bitcoin has become the forerunner of cryptocurrencies based on a decentralized network, inspiring the emergence of new digital currencies. Tokens, cryptocurrencies and other types of digital assets that are not Bitcoin are collectively referred to as alternative coins or Altcoins. Altcoins perform various functions in the broader cryptocurrency system. For example, Litecoin processes blocks every 2.5 minutes, making it four times faster than Bitcoin. Cardano, on the other hand, was developed to support the creation of decentralized financial applications (dApps), thus competing with Ethereum.

Large increases in the Altcoin market are being referred to as the Altseason. Websites specializing in cryptocurrency market capitalization rankings, such as Coinpaprika.com, for instance, report that there are tens of thousands of Altcoins in 2022.

THE PROBLEMS OF CRYPTOCURRENCIES

Let's take a look at the five largest cryptocurrencies in the context of the issues that are giving the investors around the world sleepless nights.

Let's take the oldest cryptocurrency, Bitcoin, under the magnifying glass. It is characterized by old technology, now 13 years old, high energy consumption required for mining, expensive transactions and no significant development or friendly interface.

Bitcoin has never undergone a security audit which can lead to serious errors or extortions. During its short history, there have already been two inflation bugs allowing a person who found a bug in the code to mint any quantity of Bitcoins, which would cause the collapse of the cryptocurrency, and perhaps the collapse of the entire market.

In the first case, the Blockchain was rewound with the consent of the miners, thus getting rid of the illegally minted coins. In the second case, the bug discoverer reported it voluntarily and did not exploit it for disreputable purposes. While both bugs have been corrected, the question still remains: how many more of them could be in the Bitcoin code? A security audit could resolve any doubts on this point.

On the other hand Ethereum's major problem is its low scalability, making ETH a victim of its own success. Ethereum's overloaded network has resulted in high transaction fees that have reached thousands of dollars. Nor is there any optimism in one of the founder's recent interviews, Vitalik Buterin, who said that the full implementation of Ethereum 2.0, which could theoretically solve these problems, could take another six years. Ethereum's transition from Proof of Work to Proof of Stake in September 2022, as predicted, did not raise network capacity or reduce transaction fees.

Binance Coin (BNB) is a cryptocurrency issued by the popular Binance trading platform. BNB is a utility token that can be used on the Binance exchange.

Every quarter, Binance uses one-fifth of its profits to repurchase and permanently destroy or burn the BNB coins in its vault. Initially, the coin was based on the Ethereum network.

In April 2020, Binance Capital Mgmt. bought CoinMarketCap, the largest cryptocurrency ranking service, which in itself is a conflict of interest. Binance manipulates data from various Blockchains, manually setting the ranking of certain cryptocurrencies on CoinMarketCap. There is at least one class action lawsuit filed by investors, which is not a good sign neither for Binance, nor their cryptocurrency BNB.

Cardano (ADA) is one of the largest Blockchains that uses a Proof of Stake mechanism. Research shows that it is a ghostchain, meaning that regardless of its functionality, it is not actually used or developed. Cardano uses the Haskell programming language and many developers are reluctant to work on it for this reason. Another problem for Cardano is the failure to implement smart contracts in September 2021. Furthermore, the first decentralized application implemented in Cardano is criticized due to poor performance caused by network congestion.

Created in 2013, the XRP cryptocurrency gained popularity in the bull market of 2017 and 2018. This was accompanied by significant price increases for the cryptocurrency from $0.2 to $3, following the promise of its use by major banks and money transfer networks such as Western Union and Money Gram. Unfortunately, the future has shown that no major financial institution uses XRP for money transfers and, due to the activities of XRP's founders, the value of the coins continues to fall. To make things worse, the company is entangled with legal proceedings with the US Securities and Exchange Commission, which filed a lawsuit against it in 2020. At the stake was an allegation that XRP raised $1.3 billion in unregistered securities based on digital assets by issuing XRP tokens. The prosecutors claim that XRP is not a currency, but a type of security, and is therefore subject to the strict regulations associated with it.

4 MAJOR BIGGEST CRYPTOCURRENCY SCAMS THAT LED TO $4.5 BILLION LOSSES

The growth of the cryptocurrency business in recent years has contributed to an increase in fraud. Interestingly, criminals do not use new and sophisticated methods at all, but rely on old , battle-proven and tested practices.

Bitconnect

By far the largest example of fraud is Bitconnect. Its founder, Satish Kumbhani, was accused by the US Department of Justice for, inter alia, setting up a Ponzi scheme (a financial pyramid) through a Lending Scheme. The accusation included charges of committing wire transfer fraud, commodity price manipulation and international money laundering. Originally, Bitconnect was supposed to guarantee investors a 40% return on their investment. Ultimately, Kumbhani received approximately $2.4 billion from investors and disappeared with the money. He is still wanted to this day.

Pincoin

Another major scam that rocked the cryptocurrency world was Pincoin. This Vietnamese digital currency raised around $870 million from 32,000 people. The problem with Pincoin was that instead of being paid back in cash, investors were given tokens called iFan. Unfortunately, it was not long before Pincoin's founders fled with all the investors' money.

ACChain

Chinese ACChain raised $80 million from investors but it soon became clear that there was something wrong with this cryptocurrency. Photographs of the headquarters, which turned out to be just an empty room, leaked to the public and at the same time the company disappeared without a trace along with the money stolen from investors.

Plexcoin

This scam was highly publicized because the company behind Plexcoin was shut down by the US Securities and Exchange Commission (SEC) which ordered it to return a large portion of the scammed money out of a total of $20 million. The cryptocurrency initially promised investors a return of 1,354% but this turned out to be just an empty slogan used as a bait .

These scams are just the tip of the iceberg. Every month there are new incidents that reverberate throughout the cryptocurrency world. It should be noted that Ronin Network lost $624 million, Wormhole $326 million and BeansTalk $181 million.

FAMOUS HACKS THAT SHOOK THE CRYPTO INDUSTRY

The cryptocurrency business is vulnerable to hacking of blockchains, exchanges or individual wallets. The root causes are poor security, lack of security audits and undesirable user behavior.

Mt. Gox

This is the largest cryptocurrency hacking and has become a kind of benchmark. Mt. Gox was a Japanese bitcoin exchange headquartered in Shibuya, Tokyo, which operated from July 2010 to February 2014. It handled more than 70% of all bitcoin transactions worldwide, making it the largest intermediary for bitcoin transactions. Unfortunately, the cryptocurrency trading leader's story ended with a spectacular hacking into its faulty computer system that led to the suspension of its operations, the closure of its website and service and the filing for bankruptcy protection from creditors.

In April 2014 the liquidation proceedings began. The hacked assets totaled 850,000 Bitcoins belonging to the customers and the company, which were stolen, the equivalent of more than $450 million. 200,000 Bitcoins were later recovered, but the reasons for the disappearance of the skyrocketing amount have never been explained.

Poly Network

Poly Network is an interoperability protocol for Blockchain, allowing tokens to be exchanged from one digital ledger to another, such as Bitcoin to Ether. In August 2021, Poly Network was hacked for the amount exceeding $611 million, the largest hacking in the history of cryptocurrencies until March 2022.

BitMart

One of the most trusted cryptocurrency trading platforms has lost $196 million. The money was hacked from two wallets on two Blockchains: Ethereum and BSC. Interestingly, once rumors of the hacking began to circulate online, BitMart administrators dismissed rumors of the theft. It was only some time later that BitMart CEO, Sheldon Xia, announced that the withdrawal was due to a security breach and announced that withdrawals had been temporarily suspended until further notice.

Compound

Compound was a platform for borrowing and lending cryptocurrency and earning interest. Users joined groups there, contributing their funds to the network, and these liquidity pools were used to make loans. The whole process was supervised by an algorithm that controlled it and selected the commission depending on which cryptocurrency was in short supply. Due to the platform's faulty algorithm, as much as $90 million went to randomly selected platform users. This happened during an upgrade of one of the contracts but customers' money was not affected. However, the fund that was supposed to reward providers of liquidity to the network was depleted. Robert Leshner, the head of the project, asked users to return the erroneously paid commission and offered an option of keeping a 10% finder's fee.

It is worth following the website www.rekt.news/leaderboard/ which contains a fairly comprehensive and regularly updated list of cryptocurrency hacks. As of January 2022, the list included 70 projects hacked between 2020 and 2022 for the total amount exceeding a billion dollars!

THE MOST COMMON TYPES OF CRYPTOCURRENCY SCAMS

The aim of a cryptocurrency scam is to steal investors' money, which ends with the fraudulent owner fleeing and shutting down the business. Digital currency scams are usually characterized by the creation of low-effort projects to build the image of a promising project. In reality, it turns out to be a shell corporation and there is no real value behind such a project and no way to make money from the investment.

The world of cryptocurrencies is vulnerable to extortion due to the lax regulation of its operations. Due to decentralized control, project management is concentrated in private hands which attracts all sorts of fraudsters and hackers to the industry. Projects set up to scam money often closely resemble those of honest investments and initially see increases in value, which is a magnet for new investors. Eventually, the money invested disappears in thin air along with the project owners.

TYPES OF CRYPTOCURRENCY SCAMS

Liquidity theft

This is the most common cryptocurrency scam. How does the fraud mechanism work? The originator of the project lists the Altcoin on a decentralized exchange, linking it to a best-selling cryptocurrency such as Ethereum (ETH). To make sure that the project is successful, a liquid currency must be provided and enough currency must be listed on the exchange. The next step is to promote heavily the digital currency on the Web and social media to stir investors' interest. This results in large token sales and thus a significant increase in the value of the digital currency which attracts new investors. At the peak of the token price hike, the founder withdraws all ETH from the liquidity pool, leaving investors stripped of their worthless tokens. In this manner, the founder deprives the currency of all the value contributed to it by investors, which leads to the price falling to zero and the founder disappears with the ETH tokens listed on the exchange.

Technical manipulation

The second flagship type of scam is technical manipulation which involves blocking the ability to sell investors' tokens immediately after purchasing them. Thus, the investor is deprived of the basic rights, i.e. to buy, sell, convert or spend tokens in any way he or she wishes. Sometimes these operations are only possible against the currency founder, an entity or a person of his or her choice. The dishonest founder waits until the value of the token has peaked and then sells all the tokens, disappearing once and for all from investors' sight along with all the money.

Cash withdrawals by owners

Cash withdrawal by owners is a perfectly legal practice. However, if a digital currency has been created to defraud investors, cashing out then qualifies as a criminal offence.

In this type of scam, the owner lures the investors with the benefits of the platform under construction, promising attractive functionalities that will enable them to make handsome profits in the future. Investors are fooled by the platform's marketing, investing their funds into digital currency. This boosts the value of the venture, and the founder monetizes the shares or funds (either one-off or gradually), leaving investors with worthless tokens.

Dumping

Dumping is the economic policy of selling products at prices lower than the cost of production or selling abroad at prices lower than in the domestic market.

In relation to cryptocurrencies, this phenomenon involves the rapid sell-off of large quantities of tokens by owners of a digital currency leading to a coin price plunge.

As a result, investors are left in possession of worthless tokens. Dumping is preceded by an intensive advertising campaign on the Web or social media channels. The mere buying and selling of one's own digital currency is neither prohibited nor unethical, being of a lower caliber practice than liquidity theft or technical manipulation.

SUMMARY

- Cryptocurrencies are virtual currencies that have no physical form and are based on a distributed ledger system.
- Records of cryptocurrency transaction processes are stored on the Blockchain, a digital ledger, which is a type of database developed to secure transaction records.
- Blockchain technology was first used during the implementation of the Bitcoin cryptocurrency.

- Cryptocurrencies are developed in various ways. One method of obtaining them is through Proof of Work (PoW) also known as the process of mining cryptocurrencies by miners.

- The second method of cryptocurrency acquisition is Proof of Stake (PoS), an alternative mechanism for verifying transactions and creating new blocks on the Blockchain.

- The key advantage of cryptocurrencies is profit generation. Many people have made fortunes in this business. Cryptocurrency markets were worth $3 trillion by the end of 2021.

- Bitcoin (₿) is the first decentralized digital currency that is independent of central banks, administrators or financial institutions and can be transferred directly between users without any intermediaries.

- Bitcoin was invented by a software developer (or his team), Satoshi Nakamoto, in 2009.

- Ethereum is a runner-up blockchain and cryptocurrency in terms of market capitalization following Bitcoin.

- Tokens, cryptocurrencies and other types of digital assets that are not Bitcoin are collectively referred to as alternative coins, or Altcoins.

- High price hikes in the altcoin market are called Altseason.

- Cryptocurrencies are corrupt Bitcoin is old, slow and expensive to use. Ethereum has become a victim of its own success, making transaction costs insurmountable for many users. Binance Coin is owned by a company known for market manipulation. Cardano is a Ghostchain that few people use and XRP is in court with the US SEC.

- The growth of the cryptocurrency business in recent years has contributed to an increase in fraud.

- The cryptocurrency industry is vulnerable to hacking of blockchains, cryptocurrency exchanges or individual wallets.

CHAPTER 4
THE MOST INFLUENTIAL PEOPLE IN THE CRYPTOCURRENC Y INDUSTRY

*The people that improve the world
the most often come from a place of
fulfillment. If I wish to live in a
better world, it's in my best interest
to see more people's cups full.*
Richard Heart

The problems, scams, hackings or evidence
of corruption described in the previous
chapter are the tip of the iceberg of

incidents that have taken place in the cryptocurrency business. If the invention of cryptocurrencies was the first financial revolution of our times, it looks like we need a second one to uproot bad projects, expose fake influencers and get rid of dishonest founders who develop new digital currencies just to scam investors.

Every revolution requires a strong, charismatic, honest leader who will lead people on a mass scale. So let us take a closer look at some of the most influential people in the cryptocurrency business and see if any of them is in the possession of what it takes to lead the Second Crypto Revolution.

SATOSHI NAKAMOTO

The Bitcoin founder is also one of the cryptocurrency business' most mysterious figures. It is most likely a pseudonym used by one person or a group of developers who are responsible for the development of the first cryptocurrency. Satoshi Nakamoto does not reveal his identity and gives very little information about himself, which is why he can be described as a ghost man.

By spreading an aura of mystery around himself, Nakamoto has contributed to the development of numerous conspiracy theories about himself which claim, among other things, that the founder of Bitcoin is a government organization. Some sources claim that Satoshi Nakamoto is a 37 year old Japanese man who is very smart and knows economics and cryptography well. The analysis of Bitcoin's code by experts has shown that it was not written by a professional, so it is suspected that Nakamoto was a student while working on the cryptocurrency. Nakamoto used fluent English in emails or public posts including traces of American and British English, so either he was deliberately misleading the public or it is a group of individuals.

The fact is that Nakamoto is responsible for developing the first Blockchain.

Nakamoto has never revealed his identity but has commented on traditional and fractional reserve banking on more than one occasion.

Security researcher Dan Kaminsky said Nakamoto is a team of people or a genius. In contrast, Laszlo Hanyecz, who was corresponding with Nakamoto, felt that the code was too well designed for one person. Gavin Andresen, a developer working with Bitcoin, said about the founder: he was a brilliant coder, but he was weird.

Nakamoto owns between 750,000 and 1,100,000 Bitcoin, making him the owner of $73 billion in assets, making him the 15th richest person in the world (as at November 2021). Nakamoto's activity stopped immediately after the implementation of Bitcoin. There is no traffic visible in his wallets and he does take floor in public discussions. One can conclude that he has either withdrawn from public life and professional activity or is dead. Thus, there is no indication that he is about to return and save the cryptocurrency world from the ailments plaguing it.

VITALIK BUTERIN

Vitaly Dmitriyevich (Vitalik) Buterin was born on 31 January 1994 and is a Russian-Canadian software developer and writer who made a name for himself developing the Ethereum cryptocurrency. He was born in Russia and emigrated to Canada with his parents at the age of six. He was an exceptionally gifted student, showing an interest in mathematics and programming. Even as a child, he could add three-digit numbers in his mind twice as fast as his peers. When he won a bronze medal at the

International Olympiad in Informatics (IOI) in 2012, he was struck with the idea of developing his own cryptocurrency. This idea found an outlet in Ethereum Whitepaper, which he wrote in late 2013.

Vitalik Buterin's career took off while studying at the University of Waterloo where he was awarded a $100,000 scholarship. Buterin decided to spend it not on his studies but on developing his own crypto project. He started work on Ethereum on a full scale. Buterin wrote articles about Bitcoin on the Web and was later hired to work as a member of Bitcoin Magazine editorial staff. He began his career as a publicist. Later he started to cooperate with Bitcoin Weekly and Ledger. In 2014, he developed Ethereum successfully. Vitalik Buterin's team members included Charles Hoskinson, Gavin Wood, Joe Lubin, Anthony Di Lorio and Mihai Alise. Despite allegations of owning the majority of ETH, the Ethereum founder disclosed that he holds no more than 0.9% of his digital currency.

Today, Vitalik Buterin is not only the brilliant founder of the Ethereum platform but also one of the most prominent cryptocurrency experts whose views are taken into account and respected. However, Buterin is not a businessman so he is unable to communicate his thoughts clearly and lucidly, which makes him unsuitable to lead the Second Crypto Revolution.

RICHARD HEART – A GENIUS WHO CHANGED THE WORLD OF CRYPTOCURRENCIES

Richard Heart (actually Richard Schueler) was born on 9 October 1979 in the USA. He is a businessman, author of the personal development book entitled SciVive and Fix The World, YouTuber and philanthropist. As a well-known speaker, he frequently appears on television, podcasts and video interviews where he shares his knowledge of cryptocurrencies, entrepreneurship, marketing and finance. Heart has been a guest of programs or featured in news articles on CNBC, Forbes, Business Insider, Kitco, Economic Times, CoinTelegraph and others. On his YouTube channel, he shares a wealth of expert knowledge to help viewers avoid scams, especially in the field of cryptocurrencies.

From an early age, Richard Heart was an exceptional child with an above-average intelligence quotient (IQ). He learnt to read as early as the age of three and after two days of attending primary school, his teachers found that he was years ahead of other children in terms of intelligence. As a result, he was enrolled in a school for the gifted, which was characterized by an accelerated teaching mode. In junior high school, Heart was enrolled in a program for advanced learners developed by an MIT graduate in Davie, Florida called MEGSSS (Math Education for Gifted Secondary School Students). During his time in the program, he learned such advanced topics as syllogistic inference, modus ponens and modus tollens. He quickly became interested in computer science, learning at MEGSSS to program in Scheme, the world's most powerful programming language. He was an exceptionally smart kid who absorbed knowledge like a sponge.

His father repaired air conditioners and distributed newspapers. As a young boy, Richard helped him with both of these jobs. Richard refers to this work as hard because he had to do it in the heat, it was physically strenuous and often required working alone, where you couldn't talk with anyone. These work experiences later made Richard very sociable and he enjoyed talking to people.

Richard took his first steps in business as a teenager, setting up a home-based car stereo business. With Heart's love of entrepreneurship, it was not long before he founded an e-commerce platform, an air conditioner manufacturing company and a sex shop.

The following years brought him not only new business experience but also his first major financial successes. Heart set up a mortgage lending company, a business dealing with website optimization from the perspective of Web browsers. The latter company became the golden goose bringing in a turnover of $60 million a year.

Heart's business success led him to retire in the early 2000s. At that time, he came across Bitcoin via Reddit which led to his interest in cryptocurrencies. The fruit of his interest in Bitcoin was the development of HEX, the first Blockchain Certificate of Deposit.

HEX has provided millions of dollars in return to many active investors. As a result of this success and in compliance with his philanthropic ideals, Richard developed PulseChain – an , energy-efficient, faster and cheaper version of Ethereum. PulseChain supports the medical research organization SENS.org and raised as much as $27 million for charitable causes before its launch. Heart's youngest child is PulseX, a decentralized bitcoin exchange on PulseChain platform.

A man who inspired thousands of people to change their lives

Even in the earliest YouTube videos, you can see what Heart cared about from the very beginning – to inspire people to change. In his videos and speeches, he urged people to quit their addictions (drinking, gambling, video games) or invest in medical research. He has helped thousands of people improve their livelihoods and even make millions.

Richard shares his knowledge to help people make money on cryptocurrencies. The holders of over 300,000 Bitcoins have minted huge amounts of HEX for free. Heart educates on stopping gambling/speculation, using security-controlled software or cryptocurrency fraud.

He is considered a visionary because he predicted Bitcoin's value at $20,000 per coin at a time when its price was just $5,000. He also predicted that $20,000 would be the highest price Bitcoin would be able to reach during the 2017/2018 bull market.

Similarly, he predicted the end of the BTC bull market at almost $70,000 in May 2021, while other influencers claimed that the price of Bitcoin would rise to at least $100,000 later that year.

His YouTube channel host a myriad of videos that cover important, inspiring topics like the need for consensus in politics, convince people to make videos on a positive note, advice on business start-ups, promote medical research, advice on how to be happy or how to fix democracy.

In one of his speeches, Richard Heart disclosed his vision of building a vertically integrated crypto ecosystem. It will consist of HEX: the First Blockchain Certificate of Deposit, PulseChain which is an energy efficient, faster and cheaper version of Ethereum, and PulseX – the largest crypto exchange on the new Blockchain. Heart also mentioned that the new ecosystem will also require a wallet in the future and a method for depositing and withdrawing money between it and traditional banks. And when all these components are in place, Richard Heart will be the founder of a new cryptocurrency ecosystem independent of Ethereum, Bitcoin and the exchanges currently operating in the market.

'I'm not fucking around. I'm here to take over' – he said in his final conclusions

SUMMARY

- The problems, scams, hackings or evidence of corruption described in the previous chapter are the tip of the iceberg of incidents that have taken place in the cryptocurrency industry. If the invention of cryptocurrencies was the first financial revolution of our times, it looks like we need a second one to uproot bad projects, expose fake influencers and get rid of dishonest founders who create new digital currencies just to scam investors.

- Every revolution requires a strong, charismatic, honest leader to attract people on a mass scale . Who will become that leader?

- Satoshi Nakamoto, the Bitcoin founder, is also one of the most mysterious figures in the cryptocurrency industry.

- Immediately after Bitcoin's implementation, Nakamoto's activity ceased. One does not see any movement in his wallets and he does participate in public debates. One can conclude that he has either withdrawn from public life and professional activity or is dead. Thus, there is no indication that he is about to return and save the cryptocurrency world from the ailments plaguing it.

- Vitalik Buterin is the Russian-Canadian software developer who designed Ethereum. Today, Vitalik Buterin is not only the brilliant founder of the Ethereum platform, but also one of the most prominent cryptocurrency experts whose views are taken into account and respected.

- Buterin, however, is not a businessman and does not know how to communicate his thoughts clearly and lucidly, so he is not fit for the position of the Second Crypto Revolution leader.

- Richard Heart is an entrepreneur, author of the personal development book entitled

SciVive and Fix The World, YouTuber and philanthropist.

- Richard Heart is building a new cryptocurrency ecosystem independent from Ethereum, Bitcoin and the exchanges that currently operational in the market.
- His track record and incredible vision make him the best candidate to lead the Second Crypto Revolution.

PART II

THE SECOND CRYPTO REVOLUTION

CHAPTER 5
HEX: THE FIRST BLOCKCHAIN CERTIFICATE OF DEPOSIT

Two things matter in
cryptocurrencies:
price appreciation and security.
Richard Heart

Having achieved financial success in business in 2003, Richard Heart retired. In 2011, he became interested in cryptocurrencies. At that time he mined full blocks of Bitcoin, which included as many as 50 Bitcoins. As a serial businessman, he decided to create a new cryptocurrency as an alternative to banking products. Analyzing the financial markets, Richard noticed that Certificates of Deposit were the most popular product of banks. Their value in the USA and China reached $7.2 trillion at the time, making this market 50% larger than the cash market that Bitcoin was addressing. The conclusions of his analysis, combined with his business experience and acumen, inspired Richard to develop the world's first Certificate of Deposit based on Blockchain technology.

The origins of HEX can be traced back to November 2018, when Richard Heart first publicly began talking about the BitcoinHEX project. The product was launched on 2 December 2019 under the name HEX, announcing a nearly year-long launch phase.

The product could be purchased in the open market or ETH could be converted into HEX through a mechanism known as the Adoption Amplifier (AA for short). A temporary single-level referral program was also introduced to attract as many users as possible.

Bitcoin holders were able to claim HEX tokens for free. Owners of more than 300,000 BTC worth tens of billions of dollars in more than 30,000 different wallets minted their own HEX using a smart contract. The system awarded 10,000 HEX for 1 BTC, with the amount decreasing each day.

All unclaimed HEX tokens on the last day of the launch phase called BigPayDay were distributed to stakers, i.e. investors who staked their money for even one day. This day marked the end of the opportunity to receive free HEX for Bitcoin holders, the AA program and the referral program. The distribution process was designed to ensure that the holders of the most HEX staked for the longest period receive the most HEX and that they can maintain the price in the future by not selling their tokens for a long period of time.

According to Richard Heart, the main advantage of HEX over Bitcoin is that the platform was developed 10 years later, allowing it to learn from its predecessor's mistakes.

The second differentiator that makes HEX superior to Bitcoin is the idea of creating an ambitious product to replace the most popular banking product, creating the world's first cryptocurrency Certificate of Deposit

HEX's innovation, successes and tremendous growth over its first years in the market have earned it many critics, accusing HEX of being a scam or fraud.

In 2020 HEX achieved 140 times higher growth than that of the prototype developed by Satoshi Nakamoto. After the first two years of smooth performance and a 10,000-fold increase in price, the first cryptocurrency experts are starting to like HEX, although many still do not admit it.

WHAT IS HEX?

HEX is the first Blockchain Certificate of Deposit (CD) in the cryptocurrency ecosystem, the banking equivalent of a term deposit. By investing in HEX, instead of going to a bank and putting dollars or euros on deposit account, you stake your funds in the form of HEX tokens using a smart contract. The investment must last between 1 day and 5555 days (15.2 years). At the end of the selected time, you recover your funds with your profits. You can buy tokens by exchanging other cryptocurrencies for HEX. Then, through the go.hex.com/stake website, you stake a certain amount of tokens for the selected period.

Staking tokens is completely voluntary and optional. Alternatively, you can simply buy and hold HEX in your wallet without interacting further with the HEX contract. Assuming the price of the token rises in the long term, you will one day be able to sell it at a higher price. However, no interest will be accrued while you wait.

There are two key differences that should be mentioned here between a traditional term deposit in a bank and a HEX contract. In a bank, you save let us say, $1,000 for a period of seven years. You receive an average of 1% interest per annum for this, meaning that after 7 years there is a total amount of $1072 in your account. Unless the bank goes bankrupt or some other drastic and unpredictable story happens, you are guaranteed to get your $1072 back. Using the HEX contract, you buy HEX tokens for a value of $1,000. Let's say you get 20,000 HEX for that because on the day of purchase the price of one HEX was $0.05. The HEX contract pays an average of 38% interest per year. So after seven years you will have 190,626 HEX. If HEX is still worth $0.05, you will have $9531. If HEX falls in value to $0.01, you will have $1906, and if HEX rises in value to $0.25, you will have $47,656. And so on... HEX guarantees you a payment of your capital and interest in HEX. So it works in the same manner as a dollar-denominated term deposit in a bank, except that the interest is much higher. However, HEX does not guarantee what its dollar value will be on the day the deposit ends. With these two elements, it fundamentally differs from a conventional term deposit with a bank.

HOW DOES HEX WORK?

Investors operate like a mint and create new coins in exchange for holding HEX on a term deposit for a set period of time. When the contract ends, the HEX contract mints new coins that repay the holder. A HEX staker is akin to a Bitcoin miner without the need to invest in expensive equipment and electricity. HEX offers an annual interest rate of around 40%, depending on the duration of the contract and the number of investors staking their money. Receiving such a high rate of return is possible if the average duration of our investment is minimum 6.6 years (as of August 2022).

High returns are possible because the rate of return offered is in HEX and not, for instance, in US dollars. A HEX deposit is therefore much more profitable than one with a traditional bank. Investors earn interest, oscillating from 3.69% (if 99% of the total supply is staked) to 369% (if only 1% of the total supply is locked in) and from the change in the price of the HEX token which, despite many even 90% temporary falls invariably shows an upward trend.

There are also no intermediaries for the Richard Heart's product, such as banks, financial institutions, governments, companies or other people. It is an independent code interacted with by a community of investors who manage the tokens and the entire ecosystem. In HEX, you are the central bank printing your own money.

HEX offers unique benefits such as true ownership, divisibility, convertibility, anonymity, relatively easy storage, very easy tradability or resistance to inflation. HEX was developed by the software developers who created Ethereum's code and fixed its bugs, resulting in higher quality code that is a single, permanent, smart Blockchain-based contract. Even if Richard Heart dies, this will not stop HEX and it will continue to operate. There is no central entity in control of HEX, you are the true owner of your HEX with your private keys.

HEX FOR TECHNOPHOBES

Surely you already know something about Bitcoin and other cryptocurrencies. HEX is like a better bitcoin. It works like a spreadsheet that records how much HEX each investor has. By owning HEX, you have your own password to use it, just like you have a PIN for your ATM card. You can freeze your HEX for a period of your choice, similar to a term deposit at your bank. At the moment you can earn about 38% per year on this. Much more than the banks offer. This interest is paid at 3.69% inflation. No one owes anyone anything. HEX has been on the market for more than 3 years and in just the first 1.5 years it has increased in value 10,000 times. There is no indication that it cannot do this again. It has outperformed bitcoin in its first 2 years of existence.

HOW TO MAKE MONEY WITH HEX?

There are two ways to make money from HEX: you can buy tokens in order to hold them and sell them at a future profit or stake them in a long-term deposit and receiving a guaranteed return on your investment. Staking is nothing more than freezing a certain amount of HEX tokens, which works in the same manner as a term deposit, only that it operates in the cryptocurrency ecosystem. You can stake tokens for a period of between 1 and 5555 days.

How does it work? It's simple. I stake, for instance, 10 000 HEX for one year. For the duration of the contract I cannot withdraw the funds under threat of financial penalty, quite like in the case of a traditional bank deposit. When the term expires, the investment ends and I receive back my 10 000 HEX tokens and the return on my investment. This is perhaps the first of the financial products ever to be frozen for a period of 15 years, with deposits worth many billions of dollars. The average length of a HEX staking is almost seven years! HEX is an economic breakthrough worthy of a Nobel Prize.

Stakers receive HEX on a daily basis, although they cannot withdraw it until the end of the agreement they signed with the HEX contract. The system automatically calculates how much HEX our investment generated over the last 24 hours. Once the stake is over, the system user can unstake his or her coins and sell them at the current price, hold them while waiting for a better price on the market or stake them again.

HEX has a lower inflation rate than Bitcoin, even after Bitcoin halved its inflation rate twice in its first 10 years of existence. HEX's inflation rate fell to less than 3.69% within a year, while it took Bitcoin more than 10 years. HEX stakers are paid out of inflation and can maintain its price through staking. Bitcoin miners earn money by selling the coins they mine, which lowers the price of BTC. Bitcoin miners donate money to companies that produce equipment or electricity, much to the detriment of the environment. HEX investors earn far more in interest from their investments than the rate of inflation. For HEX stakers inflation is a benefit, not a cost.

The distinguishing feature of HEX is that the stakers mint their own rewards. This results in a situation where the investor becomes indebted to himself or herself because there are no intermediaries in the HEX system. The investor himself or herself runs the code to mint his or her own rewards. The strength of HEX is its users because token is created thanks to them. It is worth noting that mining rewards are dynamic and similar to those in Bitcoin. Rewards in HEX are paid out regardless of whether the currency records a decline or an increase. The investor does not have to worry about whether he or she will receive it. Funds for payouts are taken from a pool that depends on our shares in the overall system. The payout is based on your shares divided by their total number in the system.

An important aspect of HEX is receiving a bonus which significantly increases the return on investment because it is much easier to receive a 40% bonus than to buy 40% more Bitcoins. Breaking a contract before time results in a penalty imposed by the system. This can amount to only losing some or all of the profit generated or even the entire amount invested! This depends on the length of the contract and when it was broken. This is part of the so-called truth mechanism. If you declare that you want to stake funds for, let's say, 3 years, then keep your word and do not break the contract after one year or suffer the consequences. Penalty funds in the form of HEX tokens are added to the payout pool at the end of the contract. For example, a contract is terminated ahead of schedule and a penalty of 10 000 HEX is imposed. The interest pool for investors is increased by half of this amount or in this case 5000 HEX. The other half goes to the so-called Origin Address, a crypto wallet linked to the HEX launch. The contract accumulates a payout pool each day. The payout pool is based on a daily inflation of 0.009955% of the total coin supply. This gives 3.69% over 52 weeks with the interest rate calculated daily. At the end of the contract, it accumulates the total payout from your holdings and withdrawals for the entire investment period. The contract mints the HEX and credits them to your account.

HEX FOR FIVE YEAR OLDS

Do you know what dollars look like, right? You can use them to buy all sorts of cool things, such as chocolate cookies. Suppose one cookie costs $1. Some very powerful people decided one day that they would print a lot more dollars. This is called 'inflation' and there is nothing you can do to stop it. So we now have twice as many dollars but a single dollar is only worth half of what it used to be. Now you need $2 to buy one cookie.

To make sure you can buy as many cookies as you want in the future, you should invest your dollars. HEX is one way to do this. If you had bought some HEX 2 years ago with your $1, you would have $10,000 today. You could buy an awful lot of chocolate cookies with that!

IS HEX SAFE?

HEX has undergone two independent security audits by reputable companies - chainsecurity.com and coinfabrik.com and one economic audit. All three audits were passed and the auditors found no gross irregularities. HEX's security is governed by a code that cannot be modified which sets it apart from many other cryptocurrencies. The HEX code is public and anyone can verify it.

Bitcoin had two bugs that allowed any number of free Bitcoins to be minted. The first bug minted 184,000,000,000,000 BTC, making Andresen and Nakamoto remove the transaction from the block and roll back the Blockchain. The next error was discovered by a Bitcoin Cash developer. Thanks to his honesty, it was possible to fix the error, which could have resulted in the collapse of Bitcoin and perhaps the entire cryptocurrency system.

HEX is up and running and error-free which also translates into its model security. It should be noted that the HEX website has never been hacked. If, for instance, the main interface for staking, go.hex.com/stake, ceased to exist, this would not affect the functioning of HEX because users can interact with the contract through multiple independent interfaces.

HEX is an icon of security in the crypto industry.

REVOLUTIONARY MARKETING

It is worth noting that HEX stood out from the start with its carefully planned branding, that is brand identity. The first version of the HEX.COM website was designed to look like an obvious scam. Its flashy design was meant to attract the attention of investors susceptible to real scams and losing money on them. Heart argued that an investor would be quicker to invest in something that sparkles like jewels than in a product that looks like a boring financial offer. This argument also fitted in with Heart's wider philosophy that such design helps to protect people from fraud. Rather than investing in a real scam, its potential victims could instead invest in HEX.

The HEX logo and name refer to the hexagon, which often appears in science fiction films. The name is short, monosyllabic and easy to pronounce and spell, so it is impossible to mispronounce. Bitcoin, on the other hand, poses problems when pronouncing and spelling the name, and can be confused with Bitscoin, Bit coins or Bit-corn. The color scheme of the HEX logo provides maximum contrast, making it stand out from other cryptocurrency sites. The three hexagons in the logo symbolize the growth of the investment, and the web address HEX.COM has the same length as BITCOIN without the domain. HEX is not a company, so it does not have a marketing department and does not run standard advertising campaigns.

Thanks to HEX, hundreds of people have become millionaires or even billionaires, swapping an often mediocre life full of financial problems or a middle-class life for living in clover. This is how a community of 'Hexicans' or investors emerged. They came to trust HEX, becoming the main marketing fuel for the platform and Richard Heart's legacy. The Hexicans, carry out a lot of advertising activities that translate into growing interest in the system.

One of the community activities is the development of websites dedicated to HEX, such as: www.stakedwealth.com or www.lookintohex.com. The former site provides information on tokens, the rules of the ecosystem and there is an opportunity to receive free advice. Look Into HEX, on the other hand, is something for chart lovers. There we can, among other things, compare the return on investment in the early years of BTC, HEX, ETH, preview the current liquidity of the coin or the speed of adoption by users.

The website hexstreamers.com and www.thepulsetube.com show that there are now around 100 YouTubers who regularly make videos about HEX and Richard Heart's future projects, which is a powerful brand asset. Other community-developed sites include: hex.vision, customhex.com, hexgraphs.com, apphex.win/charts, staker.app and many others.

Richard has over 150K subscribers on Youtube and over 250K followers on Twitter. The main chat about HEX.COM on Telegram has around 50K members, and there are more channels dedicated to HEX.

Another effort by Hexicans to promote the brand was to take out HEX adverts in the London Evening Standard newspaper, The Economist magazine, on the British Underground and on buses in Birmingham. The HEX logo also began to appear on the British taxis. At a certain point of time HEX was almost everywhere, it was popping out of the fridge.

The Hexicans, without any support on the part of Richard, pooled together for a car and driver to represent HEX in the 2022 NASCAR Daytona 500 raising $600,000 in one week. At one of the car events in the USA, Lamborghini Huracan EVO in HEX colors won first place as the fastest car, reaching 375 km/h. Subsequent cars of the same brand represented HEX in local races in the UK.

Richard Heart also met with Hexicans during an organized road trip around Europe. He announced the location of the meetings at the last moment on his social media to ensure his safety. He visited, among other things, Warsaw, Prague and Amsterdam. I managed to celebrate HEX's 2nd birthday in London and had dinner with Richard Heart in exchange for financial support for the documentary 'The Highest of Stakes'. The documentary will tell the story of the HEX founder, his product and it will be a thrilling movie that makes one's blood curdle on the scale of the best thrillers[5].

One of the examples of HEX's non-standard marketing is Heart's purchase of the world's largest polished diamond called 'The Enigma'. The diamond is believed to be two billion years old. It is a 555.55 carat diamond with 55 facets. Richard renamed it to The HEX.COM Diamond. Heart bought it for $4.28 million. Judging by the publicity it gained, it is fair to say that this was a deliberate part of the promotion of HEX.COM.

In mid-2022, when it was already clear to everyone that the cryptocurrency market was in a deep slump, Richard launched a marketing campaign to outrage as many people as possible and thus draw attention to the system he was developing. The Web has been flooded with photos and videos where Richard boasts of a watch collection worth almost $10 million, new supercars from Lamborghini, Ferrari and Mercedes or branded clothes from designers such as

Versace, Louis Vuitton and Prada. In a number of speeches, he has regularly boasted that he is the proud owner of a large penis...

***

HEX is a complex product and the aforementioned introduction provides you with the key information that should be enough to get you started on the adventure of investing into this product. I described the mechanics of how it works, the methods of making profit on HEX and the security that Richard Heart's system provides. If you are interested in technicalities, details nuances or HEX /Bitcoin benchmarking analysis see HEX.COM website where you will find more detailed information.

SCAM ACCUSATIONS

Since the inception of the first cryptocurrency, the market was abound in scams because many people wanted to dishonestly cash in on the crypto business. On the other hand, every new project, even BTC or ETH, was accused of being a scam but over time the general public became convinced of the good intentions of their founders. It was no different with HEX, and the main accusations were as follows:

IS IT TOO LATE TO INVEST IN HEX?

Bitcoin has risen 6.9 million times from $0.01 to $69,000 in 12 years. Many people complained regularly that BTC was too expensive and many people did not invest in BTC for this reason. Over the years, its price has increased, reaching a skyrocketing $69,000 per token in 2021.

HEX has grown 10,000 times in less than two years and if this trend of growing faster than Bitcoin in its early years continues, it will grow at least another 650 times, making 1 HEX token worth more than $350 in 10 years. The takeaway from this forecast is that it is not too late to invest in HEX. If you do it in time, you have the chance to boost your profits significantly in the future.

ACCUSATION OF A PONZI SCHEME

A Ponzi scheme is a financial pyramid that was first used by an Italian expatriate Charles Ponzi in 1919 in the USA. The Ponzi scheme involves attracting as many investors as possible by luring them with the prospect of quick and high returns. The invested funds are not invested in assets and the profit source of the venture are the contributions of new investors. In the final phase of the Ponzi scheme payouts are equated with the founder's capital which leads to the investment collapse. This quasi-structure is usually promoted with a false magic mechanism to enhance credibility of the high rate of return. HEX is not a Ponzi scheme because the return is derived solely from inflation and not from investor contributions, which is included in the smart contract and the users creates their own rewards.

HEX has been referred to not only as a Ponzi scheme but also as a multi-level marketing (MLM) system. MLM involves referring users at multiple levels, which results in newly deposited funds being passed on to old users. The MLM scheme is similar to a Ponzi pyramid. In HEX there is no referral scheme and no intermediaries. Under the scheme you mint the rewards yourself, similar to what Bitcoin miners do.

SPECULATIVE BUBBLE

A speculative (or economic) bubble occurs when there is a sudden and continuous amplification of asset prices which attracts new investors. Let's explore the two conditions that must occur for us to speak of a speculative bubble. The first one: there must be a sudden change in the price of an asset above its average value and then this phenomenon must persist for some time. The second condition for a speculative bubble is a price adjustment, i.e. a bubble burst or crash. Any price set in the free market can be adjusted, which does not mean that the product in question must be a bubble or a Ponzi scheme. Such a trend is specific to the cryptocurrencies such as Bitcoin, Ethereum or HEX, but also to the housing market.

IS HEX A SCAM?

Accusations of fraud arose not long after the HEX product went public. Their source was the jealousy of traders or investors of Richard Heart's success. Many of the haters blackened HEX on the grounds that they had chosen not to invest in it, having watched the cryptocurrencies huge increases over the years. No one has ever been defrauded by HEX, as it is a decentralized and complete Blockchain-based product that involves tokens invested into term deposits that yield a guaranteed profit. This profit comes from a fixed annual inflation rate of 3.69%. No one owes anyone anything. Each investor strikes his or her own rewards and is indebted to himself or herself, and no intermediary is involved in transactions or operations using the HEX contract. The value of HEX is practically lent to all unlocked coins when they are staked, similar to futures deposits. If HEX is a scam, where are the victims?

SUMMARY

- The origins of HEX can be traced back to November 2018, when Richard Heart first started to talk publicly about the BitcoinHEX project.

- The product was launched on 2 December 2019 under the name HEX, announcing a nearly one-year launch phase.

- HEX is the first Blockchain-based Certificate of Deposit in the cryptocurrency ecosystem, whereas its banking equivalent is a term deposit.

- By investing in HEX, instead of going to the bank and paying dollars or euros to set up a deposit, you stake your funds in the form of HEX tokens under a smart contract.

- Staking tokens is completely voluntary and optional. Alternatively, you can simply buy and hold HEX in your wallet without interacting further with the HEX contract.

- Investors mint new coins in exchange for holding HEX on a term deposit for a set period of time. When the contract life comes to an end, the HEX contract creates new coins that are used as repayment to the holder.

- The HEX staker resembles a Bitcoin miner, however, with no need to invest into expensive equipment and electricity.
- You can make money on HEX in two ways: you can buy tokens and hold them, sell them at a profit in the future or you can stake them, i.e. freeze the funds in a long-term deposit and receive a guaranteed return on your investment.
- An important aspect of HEX is receiving a bonus, which significantly increases the return on investment, as it is much easier to receive a 40% bonus than to buy 40% more Bitcoins.
- Breaking a contract prematurely results in a penalty being imposed by the system.
- HEX is a security icon. It has passed two independent audits carried out by reputable companies such as

chainsecurity.com and coinfabrik.com and one economic audit.

- The HEX logo and name refer to the hexagon that often appears in science fiction movies.
- Thanks to HEX, hundreds of people have become millionaires or even billionaires, swapping an often mediocre life full of financial problems or a middle-class life for a wealthy life.
- HEX has grown 10,000 times over the span of less than two years and if this trend of growing faster than Bitcoin in its early years continues, it will grow at least another 650 times, making one HEX token worth more than $350 in 10 years.
- HEX is not a Ponzi scheme because the profit comes solely from inflation and not from investor contributions, which is set forth in the smart contract and the users create their own rewards.
- HEX is not an MLM system because it has no referral scheme and no intermediaries.

You mint the rewards yourself, just like Bitcoin miners do.

- No one has ever been defrauded by HEX because it is a decentralized and complete Blockchain-based product that involves investing tokens in term deposits that yield a guaranteed return.

---

[5] https://www.thehighestofstakes.com/

CHAPTER 6

PULSECHAIN: A CHEAPER, FASTER, ENERGY-EFFICIENT ALTERNATIVE TO ETHEREUM

Do you want more Bitcoin? Do you want more Ethereum? You won't earn more of them simply by owning them. You need to buy them or invest in something that is rising in price faster. Then you can buy more! How

about investing in HEX or
PulseChain?
Richard Heart, Twitter

Ethereum has begun to grow larger over the years gaining popularity. This led to ever-increasing transaction fees, which became an entry and exit barrier for smaller investors. All this had negative impact on HEX and other Ethereum-based tokens.

Rather than lowering transaction fees for trading and staking HEX, the ETH improvements have led to increasing them many times. For instance, I once bought 100,000 HEX for the sum of $500, staking it for maybe $1. After a year, the value of the investment rose to $7,000, but the unstaking involved a cost of $700. Despite the sizable profit, the cost of unstaking could be considered as highway robbery.

Rising transaction fees were keeping investors awake at night and they were under no illusion that this problem would be solved before the full implementation of ETH 2.0 which could take several more years. Moreover, the more work on the second version of Ethereum progressed, the more it began to indicate that it would do nothing to reduce transaction fees. Nor did anyone expect Richard Heart to undertake efforts to address this issue.

The breakthrough came in 2021 when Richard started talking on YouTube about the issue of Ethereum upgrades and the increase in transaction fees, arguing that they were unacceptable. At the time, he first mentioned the idea of building a new Blockchain to solve this problem. Its name was not yet known at the time. Details gradually started to emerge but at the start all that was known was that Richard was building a faster, cheaper, fee-burning alternative of Ethereum.

SACRIFICE PHASE

Shortly afterwards, Richard informed about an option of investing into PulseChain. Information about the planned Sacrifice Phase was soon made public. Sacrifice Phase ran from 15 July to 3 August 2021 and was a kind of pre-sale, where users could invest in PLS tokens from a special pool. Each sacrificer received points and the number of points depended on the day on which the sacrifice was made and the dollar value of the cryptocurrency being sacrificed at the same time.

Richard Heart could not conduct a standard ICO (Initial Coin Offering) in order to raise funds for a new cryptocurrency venture because this would be considered an unregulated financial product under American law and would certainly not appeal to the US Securities and Exchange Commission. Moreover, as a multi-billionaire, he certainly didn't need extra money for his new projects either. Sacrifice Phase was his next philanthropic venture enabling people who decided to support his vision to make a lot of money.

The website www.pulsechain.com says that participation in the sacrifice is a demonstration of the user's faith that the blockchains are free speech which is a protected human right and not a means of investment. Richard treats PulseChain as a political statement of the users involved, which has no monetary value. Sacrifice was therefore not an ICO and if Richard Heart officially sought to generate profits for himself or investors, he would face severe legal consequences for doing so.

In practice, users who donated money to the sacrifice could not expect anything and knew that they may or may not make money. As a result, the SEC has no reason to launch any investigation. And while it is not hard to guess that all or almost all those who sacrificed their money were hoping to make a profit, in practice their hands would have been tied if, for instance, PulseChain had never been launched.

One way of sacrificing for PulseChain was to support the SENS.org charity which makes efforts to extend human life. People who donated not to Richard but to the SENS foundation, received PLS points just like everyone else. In total, the foundation received more than $27 million using this method. Overall, the entire sacrifice phase generated more than $700 million for PulseChain and is the largest pre-sale in crypto currency history.

The initial phase of the sacrifice was to last 19 days and it was most cost-effective to join the project during this time. After it came officially to an end, Richard decided to extend the campaign due to the large number of people who continued sacrificing. However, with each consecutive day of sacrifice, the value of each dollar sacrificed was less and less.

For the first 5 days, users had the best rate. For $1 they received 10 000 points. So if they bid $100 on days 1 to 5, they received at least 1 million points. Investing

$100 on the last day of the campaign entailed receiving at least 505,050 points, **almost** half as many.

I emphasize almost because there was a premium for the amount sacrificed. The more dollars you sacrificed compared to others, the higher your premium would be. The address that offered the most (in USD value) will receive the highest premium of 2.5x its number of points. The address that offered the least will receive 1.0x (no premium). Each user in between receives a premium between 1.0x and 2.5x.

WHAT IS PULSECHAIN?

Richard Heart's new project called PulseChain is a fast and sustainable Blockchain that is a copy of Ethereum with modified and streamlined code. PulseChain has its own native Pulse token (PLS) which those who have taken part in the sacrifice phase will receive at launch. The token will also be given for free to any user with ETH in their wallet on PulseChain's launch date. PulseChain will replicate the entire contents of a user's wallet on the Ethereum network including all tokens running on the network.

PulseChain's differentiator will be to charge much lower fees than Ethereum platform and to improve all Ethereum shortcomings to become more user-friendly and cost-effective. PulseChain will enable hundreds of transactions per second, which will be much faster than Ethereum's 13 transactions per second. PulseChain will use Proof of Stake (PoS) instead of Proof of Work (PoW) , while maintaining high transaction security and not having to use the high computing power of the Proof of Work.

The launch of PulseChain will be caused by the so-called Hard Fork of Ethereum.

This event occurs when the blockchain splits into two independent parts. A user group that does not want to support the main chain then moves to the newly created blockchain, either creating a new network or making some changes to the original network. PulseChain will create its own network, using the Ethereum network condition on the day of the split. To access new tokens on the PulseChain network, simply switch the network being in a compatible wallet (e.g. MetaMask).

PULSECHAIN FOR TECHNOPHOBES

PulseChain is a Web-based system where people can create new programs, make deals and speculate with cryptocurrencies. Pulse (PLS) is a type of money that uses the PulseChain system to make all of the above and other operations possible.

PulseChain was proposed by Richard Heart in March 2021. Many people took the opportunity to invest in the project early which was called the sacrifice phase. At the time of writing this book (September 2022), the second test version of PulseChain was running, and the release date of the official version is not yet known.

PULSECHAIN FEATURES THAT WILL MAKE THE PROJECT REVOLUTIONARY

PulseChain offers higher transaction processing rate that will not jeopardize security and provide smoother trading. The main reason for creating PulseChain was to reduce the cost of gas fees which have been and continue to be a pain in the neck for the Ethereum users. The PulseChain's transaction fees will be much lower than those on the Ethereum platform due to the Pulse's validators securing transactions for a small fee and due to no need to use large amounts of energy during the process.

The third feature of PulseChain is deflation which boosts the purchasing power of the token. The total supply of PLS is created at launch. The transaction fee is burnt in 75% which has the effect of reducing the total supply. In the future, when there are fewer PLS tokens in the market, their price will organically increase. PulseChain is a faster, cheaper and more lucrative competitor to Ethereum.

BIGGEST AIRDROP IN CRYPTOCURRENCY HISTORY

In the crypto business, airdrop is an opportunity to receive free tokens that will be sent at your address in exchange for performing a certain action. PulseChain's airdrop will be the largest such event in the history of cryptocurrencies.

There are two methods that will allow you to enhance your token holdings. The first method to enhance your coin holdings was to sacrifice accepted tokens on the Ethereum network in exchange for points then converted to Pulse (PLS) tokens.

The second method to double your wallet is to have tokens running on the Ethereum Blockchain at the PulseChain launch date. You will then receive a 1:1 copy of the tokens, which will be in PulseChain as long as they have been in a wallet for which you have private keys (e.g. MetaMask).

PRICE SPECULATION

As the PulseChain launch date approaches, the crypto community is increasingly trying to predict the launch price of the PLS token. According to Howtopulse.com, it will settle at: 0,00017-0,00054 $. Some predict that PLS tokens will see a 20-fold increase after three months, 70-fold after six months and 300-fold after 12 months. These values are very impressive, although opponents regard them as phantasmagoria.

But are these really pipe dreams? Looking at the launch history of other Blockchains....absolutely not! Ethereum went up 2858 times over the period of 6 years, Matic 1003 times over the period of 2.5 years and Polkastarter 608 times over the period of one year. Investors' predictions, taking into account the innovation of the project, may well come true.

Interest in PulseChain continues to grow, as evidenced by the presence of 65,000 future users on Telegram, well before the project was launched. This number continues to grow, which will ensure future liquidity of the platform. Project's strengths weight in favor of Richard Heart's new child: from its innovation, through the real transaction costs cutting, to the giving away of free tokens to users.

PULSECHAIN RELEASE DATE

Richard Heart keeps saying that 'software is harf' and that he has never yet managed to get the timing of a project right. It is therefore worth examining this topic. Initially, the PulseChain launch was expected to be 2-3 months after the sacrifice phase. Heart then announced that it would take another 2 months. Later, Richard announced many times that the project would have a couple of months delay. In the meantime, he launched the sacrifice phase for another project – PulseX. Then he again announced to the world that he needed 'two more weeks' and argued that 'we are so close now'.

After some time, the investment community was surprised by the news of new bugs in the code, that required corrections and a change of programming language, which of course extended the waiting time again. This was seen by many as an attempted scam, although it was said in the sacrifice phase that this was not an investment and no expectations should be held. It should be noted that the funds from the sacrifice addresses were not moved. There is still over a billion dollars hanging in the PulseChain and PulseX wallets, so investors' money is safe.

Since the end of May 2022, Richard has insisted that he would no longer give any timeframe until he knows the correct and fixed release date because he doesn't want people to get mad again when he gets it wrong. Richard livestreams on YouTube from time to time where he mentions that work is going well. In his Twitter bio, he wrote that free tokens will soon be available, indicating that the launch of PulseChain is worth waiting a little longer.

HYPOTHETICAL CAUSES OF DELAY

Delays can be due to the product complexity and it just has to take so long.

Bugs found in the code need to be fixed, which is very time-consuming. The developers may also have found opportunities to make the final product even better than originally envisaged and decided that it was better to delay it a few more weeks or even months than to launch what they have.

Another hypothesis is to avoid a flub , as has happened with other projects like Solana, which is shut down every now and then because something is not working properly. This is what Richard talks about most often in his public speeches. He claims that the product could be launched immediately but with the developers' knowledge of where the weaknesses are it would be vulnerable to hacking. Richard understandably prefers to address every known bug and launch a perfect product rather than something that is just good enough.

Another option is that Richard wants to launch the product when the crypto market bottoms and bear market officially ends. As a result, the project would start at very low prices and keep growing. Richard takes care about image and likes pretty charts. When asked directly, he denied this speculation, although it is possible that the ready-to-go product and the bottom of the market slump will coincide.

SUMMARY

- Ethereum has begun to grow in size over the years, gaining popularity. This led to ever-increasing transaction fees which have become an entry and exit barrier for smaller investors.

- In order to address this issue, Richard Heart is building a faster, cheaper, fee-burning copy of Ethereum.

- The PulseChain history started with the so-called Sacrifice Phase. The sacrifice phase lasted from 15 July 2021 to 3 August 2021 and was a kind of pre-sale phase when the users could invest in PLS tokens allocated from a special pool.

- The Richard Heart's new project called PulseChain is based on a fast and sustainable Blockchain technology that is a copy of Ethereum with modified and streamlined code.

- The PulseChain's differentiator will be much lower fees than those on the Ethereum platform and the improvement of all shortcomings to be a more user-friendly and cost-effective platform.

- PulseChain will offer higher transaction processing rates that will not jeopardize security and provide smoother trading.

- The main reason for the PulseChain development was to reduce the cost of gas fees which have been and continue to be a pain in the ass of the Ethereum users.

- The third feature of PulseChain will be deflation, which will boost the purchasing power of the token.

- PulseChain is also the largest airdrop in crypto history. In the crypto industry, an airdrop is the opportunity to receive free tokens that will be sent at your address in exchange for performing a certain action.

- The first method to enhance coin holdings was to sacrifice accepted ERC-20 tokens, in exchange for points then converted to Pulse (PLS) tokens.

- The second method to grow your wallet will be to hold tokens on the Ethereum blockchain at the PulseChain launch date.

- Some predict that PLS tokens will see a 20-fold increase after 3 months, 70-fold after 6 months and 300-fold after 12 months.

- Looking at the launch history of other Blockchains, it is possible. Ethereum went up 2858 times over 6 years, Matic 1003 times over 2.5 years and Polkastarter 608 times over 1 year. Investors' predictions, given the innovation of the project, may well come true.

- The release date for PulseChain has been postponed several times. Since the end of May 2022, Richard has consistently insisted that he would no longer give any timeframe until he knows the correct and fixed release date because he does not want people to get mad again if he gets it wrong.

CHAPTER 7

PULSEX: THE LARGEST EXCHANGE ON PULSECHAIN

In fact, we found it difficult to find any negative features associated with PulseX. Tokenomics has been very well thought out and seems to have been specifically designed to pump up the price. This fact, combined with the overwhelming confidence that people have shown so far, makes us think that in the first

*year of operations the PulseX price
could outperform UNI, CAKE and
SUSHI.*

www.howtopulse.com

Exchanges where cryptocurrencies can be traded are roughly divided into: centralized (e.g. Binance, Bitstamp Kraken) and decentralized (e.g. Uniswap, CurveFinance, PanCake Swap).

Centralized exchanges (CEX for short) are controlled by a company that holds users' assets. To start trading on a centralized exchange, users need to set up an account and verify their identity. Users place their trust in a middleman who, in theory, guarantees the security of transactions and funds deposited at the platform. The centralized exchange charges trading fees, part of which is allocated to platform maintenance and the rest represents the owner's profit.

Moreover, exchanges usually set a minimum cryptocurrency buy or exchange limits as well as minimum cryptocurrency withdrawal limits. On the CEX, the price of each currency is based on an order book consisting of buy and sell orders. To buy a certain token, select it and confirm the transaction and the exchange will show the purchased tokens in the user's account.

The main advantage of centralized exchanges is that you can transfer funds to and from your bank, so you can buy and sell cryptocurrencies for USD, EUR or GBP. Centralized exchanges offer beginners a relatively friendly way to trade and invest in cryptocurrencies.

The main disadvantage of centralized exchanges is their vulnerability to hackers. Large exchanges typically store crypto worth billions of dollars, making them a target for hackers and theft. An example of such an incident is Mt. Gox which was once the world's largest cryptocurrency exchange before it reported the theft of 850,000 Bitcoin, leading to its collapse.

Moreover, centralized exchanges often charge high transaction fees for their services and convenience which can be particularly painful when traded volumes are high .

***

Decentralized exchanges (DEX for short) are characterized by the fact that trading on them takes place directly between users under smart contract.

The benefits of decentralized exchanges include mainly higher security because the exchange does not hold its clients' assets which are kept in private wallets. The tokens are safer in the wallet and third parties (e.g. the exchange owner) do not get access to the tokens, which protects the assets from abuse or hacking.

A second benefit of DEX is decentralization, i.e. no middlemen in transactions and no need for identity verification, which guarantees greater anonymity. Another advantage is that tokens that are not present on centralized exchanges can be traded, providing an opportunity for investment diversification. The fees charged by decentralized exchanges are often lower than on centralized exchanges.

The main disadvantage of decentralized exchanges is that they do not allow the conversion of cryptocurrencies into traditional money and their transfers to/from banks, making them less convenient for users who do not already own cryptocurrencies.

Moreover, users of decentralized exchanges must securely store the keys and passwords to their crypto wallets. Otherwise, their assets are lost forever and cannot be recovered. The vast majority of crypto transactions are handled by centralized exchanges, suggesting that they account for the majority of traded volume.

Due to the lack of volume, decentralized exchanges often lack liquidity, and with low trading volumes it can be difficult to find buyers and sellers.

A BRIEF HISTORY OF DECENTRALIZED EXCHANGES

The birth of cryptocurrencies in 2009 created a new asset class in which millions of people started to invest. The emergence of centralized exchanges gave rise to new problems, such as hacking attacks, through which many people lost their funds or forced them to hand over control of their tokens to third parties. This contradicted the ideas of Satoshi Nakamoto, the founder of Bitcoin. These issues highlighted to the crypto community that decentralization must also extend to exchanges. This concept inspired many companies to start working on DEX. In 2014, NXT launched the first exchange for decentralized exchange called NXT Asset Exchange. In the following years, new exchanges were created, such as Komdo and Block DX.

The real revolution came with the launch of Uniswap at the end of 2018 which to this day is the largest decentralized exchange in terms of funds traded on it.

Uniswap is a fully decentralized software with high transaction liquidity for trading tokens on the Ethereum network. Uniswap has no order book and allows trading without intermediaries thanks to contracts built into the protocol.

Uniswap offers the highest level of decentralization and resistance to censorship. The protocol and interface of the DEX exchange were developed by Uniswap Labs. At the core of the software are liquidity providers who create the so-called liquidity pools, thereby providing liquidity to the entire platform.

PULSEX – THE FIRST DEX EXCHANGE ON THE PULSECHAIN NETWORK

Since Uniswap is the largest decentralized exchange on the Ethereum network, an exchange on the PulseChain network would also be required. Thus, PulseX was born. As was the case with PulseChain, PulseX created a collection (Sacrifice Phase) where tokens could be sacrificed even before the exchange launch. Each user received a multiplier of max. 2.5x and all those who sacrificed the most were ranked higher . In the last days of the Sacrifice Phase, the bonus factor was at its worst and the user who sacrificed tokens at that time only gained 1.75x.

PULSEX FUNCTIONS

PulseX (short for **PulseChain Ex**change) is the main exchange of the PulseChain ecosystem and a copy of the Uniswap exchange with improved features and parameters. Like other decentralized exchanges, such as SushiSwap and Uniswap, PulseX has its own token, PLSX.

PulseX enables the exchange of PLS (PulseChain) tokens for PulseX (and vice versa) and the trading of other tokens. The goal of the setting up the PulseX exchange is to trade and maintain liquidity of the ecosystem and to boost the value of tokens. The advantages of the PulseX exchange include: 4-fold the Uniswap bandwidth , the use of Proof of Stake (PoS) and a deflation mechanism that reduces the number of available PLSX tokens with each transaction.

PulseX will also be the world's largest yield farm. Yield Farming is a process that uses decentralized finance (DeFi) applications to maximize profits. Users lend crypto on the DeFi platform and earn a specific cryptocurrency in exchange for their services. Thanks to the so-called bridges between different blockchains, it is possible to exchange across chains such as Binance Chain, Ethereum or Polygon, allowing DeFi applications to become multi-blockchain and support smart contract functions. As the world's largest yield farm, PulseX works in the same manner as I described above. Each exchange of one currency for another provides the liquidity provider with a reward. In addition, PulseX users can, through chain bridges, pair their tokens in the Ethereum network with free copies in the PulseChain network to provide liquidity and profit. This action reinforces the value of the token copies they received for free.

How will new users be able to get tokens on PulseX? The first method was by sacrificing resources in the Sacrifice Phase which is now ended. For each sacrifice, users received a certain number of points, proportional to the contribution and sacrifice time, for which they are to get PLSX tokens. The second method will be the direct purchase of tokens in the free market. In addition to PulseX, there will be a second token to encourage liquidity providers. The token will be distributed as a bonus to certain liquidity providers. At the time of writing this book, its name is not known yet.

Therefore PulseX creates opportunities to profit from trading tokens or being a liquidity provider. Due to the fact that cryptocurrencies have the highest rates of return in the world, the return on investment on PulseX can be really high. PulseX provides full transparency: on the platform you will easily see which addresses are trading assets, which address has made a buy or sell transaction and how many tokens are left in its account. You will also be able to make a precise analysis of network activity.

WHAT WILL LIQUIDITY LOOK LIKE ON THE PULSEX EXCHANGE?

PulseX will be the exchange with the highest liquidity for PulseChain. The initial liquidity will come from a special program (the so-called bot) that will copy the liquidity of tokens from Uniswap,

Sushiswap and other popular exchanges at launch. Copies of these tokens will be available on PulseX, which will be joined by new PLS tokens. The best liquidity will attract a large number of investors who will create a large volume. This in turn will attract liquidity providers who make money from it. With centralized liquidity on the exchange, there will be lower fluctuations in token prices.

Fees on PulseX are lower than Ethereum or Bitcoin because it runs exclusively on PulseChain. Richard Heart's system provides a lower transaction cost (less than $0.01) and takes just three seconds to confirm!

This is a 180-degree change because Ethereum fees often cost from a few to several thousand dollars and transaction processing takes from a few minutes to a few hours.

Each transaction on PulseX incurs a fee of 0.25% in value, 0.17% goes to liquidity providers, 0.03% is transferred to the

PulseX account and for 0.05% PLSX tokens are automatically bought and burned.

It will be possible to stake with PLSX as well as with HEX tokens but without the time-lock feature.

Most likely, PulseX will release a staking pool which will be similar to those known from other Ethereum decentralized exchanges such as Pancake Swap and Cake token. PLSX will be able to be stored in MetaMask by switching networks in the wallet making all tokens visible in the wallet.

PRICE FORECASTS

HEX has been a huge success and has contributed to many investors' fortunes around the world. Richard Heart is considered by many to be a cryptocurrency genius who does not rest on his laurels, and implements an improved Ethereum: PulseChain and the decentralized PulseX exchange. Through an analysis of various factors, I will attempt to present a couple of expected price scenarios for the PLSX token.

Certainly no one can predict exactly how much one PLSX token will be worth at launch date. One can speculate on this subject, taking into account rationale and case studies of other cryptocurrency projects.

The majority of the crypto community claims that PulseX could outperform Uniswap, CAKE and SushiSwap due to its high potential because it has other superior features and innovations. The UNI token owned by Uniswap reached its lowest price of $0.4 on 17 September 2020. UNI recorded its highest price on 3 May 2021 at $45, an increase of more than 10,000%. The other token with a large increase is Pancake Swap (CAKE), which rose more than 400% from $8 to $45 in 2021.

Another phenomenal growth was recorded by SushiSwap with the SUSHI token, which rose from $0.5 to $24.

The PLSX token could achieve similar increases to several of its predecessors on other Blockchains:

- UNI - gain of 10.733% in 229 days,
- 1INCH - gain of 1.034% in 131 days,
- SUSHI - profit of 4.936% in 130 days,
- INJ - gain of 3.814% in 179 days,
- CAKE - gain of 18.829% in 173 days,
- SNX - gain of 88.306% in 772 days,
- LRC - gain of 19.285% in 694 days,
- RUNE - gain of 267.792% in 601 days.

What impact will PulseChain and PulseX have on the HEX price? At least three scenarios are possible. Already during the PulseChain's Sacrifice Phase, HEX reached an all-time high price: $0.56. After the PulseChain launch, we will have two HEXes: one will stay on the Ethereum blockchain under the name eHEX, and the other will be in the PulseChain network and we will call it HEX.

The first possible scenario will be that the prices of the two HEX tokens will reach parity. The two tokens will rise in the mid to long term, due to the upward trend of HEX and its design.

The second scenario will be an increase in HEX price on PulseChain because Richard Heart and all the people associated with the project will focus on promoting their own product independent of the Ethereum network. The eHEX price, on the other hand, will fall due to the lack of project promotion and support by Heart and other Hexicans. Even if this were to happen, although it is unlikely, investors will still not lose out. With one million HEX on the Ethereum network, they will still get one million HEX on the PulseChain network as part of the biggest airdrop ever, which will happen at PulseChain's launch date. If the PulseChain price goes up 100 times and the Ethereum price goes down

100 times or to the proverbial zero, it was still a good investment after all, looking at it in dollar terms.

Under the third and my favorite scenario, both PulseChain and PulseX will prove to be an incredible success and many early investors will make a huge amount of money from these projects. However, this will not happen without huge price volatility, which HEX on PulseChain will also be subject to. Many users under this scenario would desire to withdraw some profit and put the money they earn into something safe, not necessarily outside the cryptocurrency ecosystem. Where else would they do this if not in eHEX on the Ethereum network, a proven product that has been accruing 38% interest smoothly for more than three years? Under this scenario, PLS, PLSX and eHEX tokens would rise rapidly in value terms and HEX on PulseChain will catch up in a while. If, reading my book, you were wondering whether it was too late to invest and whether eHEX could increase another 10,000 times, you now not only know that it possible, but you also understand how.

INFLATION VS. DEFLATION

Most decentralized exchanges reward liquidity providers with fees and native tokens. In the case of some exchanges like CAKE or SUSHI, the tokens are inflationary (their supply is constantly growing). The revolutionary thing about the PLSX token is that the token will not be subject to inflation, which will translate into a reduced supply of the token in the long term. Due to the fact that PLSX token supply will decline , the coin price will show an upward trend, which is why it can outperform the aforementioned tokens.

INVESTOR BEHAVIOR

In the analysis concerning the PLS and PLSX token prices, it is important to consider the forecast of investor behavior.

Investors will apply two philosophies: they will trade in tokens or hold them time as long-term investments

Some investors will exchange PLSX for other tokens while others will stake on long-term investments. Some investors will undoubtedly combine both methods, selling some of the tokens outright and putting aside a certain pool of funds for long-term investments. For now, this is speculation based on my experience of investing into HEX and previously into other cryptocurrencies, but I cannot predict what the sentiment of PulseX users will be. The huge interest in the Sacrifice Phase which culminated in the sacrifice of around a billion dollars bodes well for the future! This is a testimony of the confidence in Richard Heart's next project, giving high hopes for the future.

It is difficult to find any snags about PulseX that would raise concern of crypto investors. PulseX's tokenomics have been well thought out and designed to make the token value grow. The combination of great tokenomics and the community's confidence in HEX means that PulseX can outperform Uniswap, CAKE and SUSHI in the first year of operations.

PulseX will be launched on a completely new chain and will be characterized by unique features. The potential to become one of the largest yield farms ever will ensure that it has a large investor base. The PulseX exchange will be highly liquid with a 'fixer bot' scheme. This will make PulseX the most widely used and liquid PulseChain exchange. Low transaction fees compared to Ethereum and Bitcoin will attract small and large investors who will use PulseX, flying to the exchange like moths to a flame. Another rationale for PulseX's success is the 10,000-fold increase of HEX price. Many digital currency developers have promised similar increases but few have succeeded.

SUMMARY

- Exchanges on which cryptocurrencies can be traded are roughly divided into: centralized (e.g. Binance, Bitstamp Kraken) and decentralized (e.g. Uniswap, CurveFinance, PanCake Swap).

- The main advantage of centralized exchanges is the ability to transfer funds to and from the bank, so buying and selling cryptocurrencies for USD, EUR or GBP.

- The main disadvantage of centralized exchanges is their vulnerability to hackers. Large exchanges typically hold cryptocurrencies worth billions of dollars making them a target for hackers and theft.

- Decentralized exchanges are characterized by the fact that trading on them takes place directly between users through under smart contracts.

- The benefits of decentralized exchanges are mainly greater security because the exchange does not hold its customers' assets, which are kept in private portfolios.

- In 2014, NXT launched its first exchange for decentralized exchange called NXT Asset Exchange.
- The real revolution came with the launch of Uniswap at the end of 2018 which to date has been the largest decentralized exchange in terms of funds traded on it.
- Since Uniswap is the largest decentralized exchange in the Ethereum network, an exchange on the PulseChain network will also be required. This is how PulseX will be born.
- As was the case with PulseChain, PulseX arranged a Sacrifice Phase during which tokens could be sacrificed even before the exchange launch.
- PulseX (short for **Pulse**Chain **Ex**change) will be the main exchange of the PulseChain ecosystem and a copy of the Uniswap exchange with improved features and parameters.
- PulseX is also the world's largest yield farm. Yield Farming is a process that uses

decentralized finance (DeFi) applications to maximize returns.

- A large part of the crypto community claims that PulseX, due to its high potential, can outperform Uniswap, CAKE and SushiSwap because it has other, superior features and innovations.

- Similarly to other decentralized exchanges, such as SushiSwap and Uniswap, PulseX has its own token - PLSX.

- The revolutionary feature of the PLSX token is that the token will not be subject to inflation, which will translate into a reduced supply of the tokens in the long term.

- Low transaction fees concerning Ethereum and Bitcoin cryptocurrencies will attract small and large investors flying to the exchange like moths to a flame.

- Another indication of PulseX's success is the 10,000-fold increase in the HEX price. Many digital currency developers have promised similar increases, but few have succeeded.

CHAPTER 8
HOW TO MAKE MONEY WITH THE SECOND CRYPTO REVOLUTION?

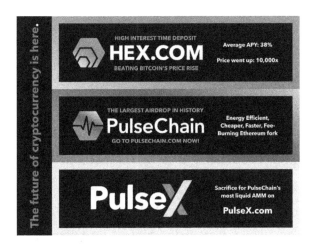

*Three types of people/institutions
make money with cryptocurrencies –*

founders, exchanges and long-term investors .
Richard Heart

If you have read my book this far, it should be clear that your future wallet should consist of four products to start with:

- (e)HEX based on the Ethereum blockchain,
- HEX based on the PulseChain blockchain
- PLS – native PulseChain token
- PLSX – native token of the PulseX exchange

In the future, I would keep a close eye on Richard Heart's next ventures, such as an incentive token for PulseX liquidity providers unnamed at the time of writing this book, a crypto wallet (alternatives to MetaMask and others), a solution for direct collaboration between traditional banks and

PulseChain network-based products and others when something is known about them. Richard once mentioned an option of setting up an investment fund, bringing together companies/organizations working on a capability of extending human life as well as setting up his own very liberal state that would follow the principles of a special economic zone.

Before you start considering a move to Hexico, in the meantime, I'll provide you with a practical step-by-step guide to the whole process of setting up accounts on cryptocurrency exchanges, buying crypto, right through to investing in the products described in the previous chapters. Take a solid sip of coffee and let's get started!

ACCOUNT ON CENTRALIZED EXCHANGE

The Bitstamp exchange is one of the largest, popular and easy-to-use cryptocurrency exchanges. There are hundreds of exchanges around the world. For the purposes of this book, I am describing how to cope on Bitstamp. On any other exchange, the process will look similar.

1. Go to bitstamp.net and click on Get Started button, which will redirect you to the form.

2. Fill in the form with your details (first name, last name, email, date of birth) and click Continue.

3. Enter the country of residence and accept the Terms and Conditions. After a while, an email will arrive in you inbox with a link to complete the registration.

4. Click on Complete Your Registration.
You will then be redirected to a form
where you create your password.
Remember to make it strong and
unique. It should have a minimum of
8 characters, upper and lower case
letters and at least one special
character.

Bitstamp

Your user ID is dg4s1616

This is also your username. You can use your User ID or your email to log in.

Get verified

Before you can start using Bitstamp, you will need to complete the following steps:

1. Enter your info and upload documents

2. Provide basic financial information

3. Enable extra security

Start Your Verification

5. Click on Start Your Verification button. You will then be redirected to the forms where you will need to enter your home address and telephone number. You will receive a code via SMS and, after entering it in an appropriate field, you will be redirected further.

6. The system will then ask you to take a photo of your document: identity card/passport or driving license. Bitstamp will guide you step by step through the process of taking and uploading your ID document photos . You will receive a link on your phone and in the app you will take a photo

of the front and reverse of the document. You will also follow the instructions provided, read the numbers off the screen and make a head movement. You will record it all and send it for verification.

7. After verification, please answer a few questions about your income and occupation and then smoothly proceed to the next verification step involving Google Authenticator. Google Authenticator is a tool for putting an extra layer of protection on your mobile app using one-time authorization codes. Using Google

Authenticator, after logging into the exchange with your username and password, you will be asked to enter a one-off code generated by the app, and only after entering it you will log into the system.

8. Once successfully verified, your account will be set up and ready to invest in cryptocurrencies. A simple and intuitive system will guide you step-by-step through all the steps of setting up your account. It takes a dozen minutes to verify your account and the entire account setting up process takes perhaps twenty minutes.

HOW CAN I DEPOSIT FUNDS IN MY BITSTAMP ACCOUNT?

The system for depositing and withdrawing funds to/from Bitstamp looks very similar on all centralized exchanges. We have a couple of options for depositing money in an account: credit/debit card, bank transfer from a bank account, cryptocurrencies, etc. Below I describe how to deposit funds in your account via a bank transfer.

1. Log into your Bitstamp account.
2. Go to Deposit tab in the top menu of the panel (third tab).
3. On the left there are the forms of payment. Select bank transfer.

4. Then select the currency and amount.
5. Click on Deposit.

6. In the next window, you will see the transfer details, the account number and the **personal number that you must enter in the title of the transfer in** order for Bitstamp to properly credit the funds to your account.

Once the deposit has been made, your funds will be credited to your Bitstamp account. The first transaction can take a few days. Remember to make the transfer from your account, where your name appears. Otherwise, the processing time can be longer or your deposit can be rejected. Once the exchange has credited your deposit, you will be able to buy your first cryptocurrencies. In the meantime, it is a good idea to set up your first wallet following the instructions below.

HOW DO I SET UP A METAMASK WALLET?

There are many wallets for handling cryptocurrencies. One of the most popular and best wallets for Ethereum and PulseChain-based products is MetaMask. Here are the steps needed to set up your first wallet:

1. Go to www.metamask.io and click on the Download button.

2. Click on Install MetaMask for Chrome assuming that you are using this browser. Other supported browsers include: Firefox, Brave and Edge.

3. On the next page, you may, but do not have to, watch a short video What is MetaMask?. I recommend doing this if these are your first steps with crypto or with this app. Click on Add to Chrome and then Add Extension.

4. For future ease of use, in the top right click on Pin to pin MetaMask permanently to your browser bar. From now on, you will see the fox icon there and can quickly access your wallet. Click on Get Started.

5. Here you may, but do not have to, consent to MetaMask processing certain information in order to improve the product.

6. On the next screen, click on Create a Wallet.

7. Here, create a new password for your MetaMask wallet. Make sure it will be unique and strong. An example of a strong password is Cartoon-Duck-14-Coffee-Glvs. It is long and

contains upper and lower case letters, numbers and special characters. Repeat the password in the Confirm Password box, tick off I have read and agree to the Terms of Conditions and click on Create.

8. On the next page, watch a short video about the Secret Recovery Phrase and carefully read the information on the right-hand side of the screen. Click on the Next button.

9. In the next step, MetaMask will show you the Secret Recovery Phrase. The Secret Recovery Phrase is a unique 12-word phrase generated when MetaMask is first set up. Your funds are linked to this phrase. If you ever lose your wallet password, the secret recovery phrase allows you to recover your wallet and funds. Keep the phrase in a safe place and you must never lose it. Click on CLICK HERE TO REVEAL SECRET WORDS.

10. Enter the phrase and click on Next. The application will take you to the next page, where you will have to re-enter the phrase following the sequence that was displayed.

11. Select the words following the sequence in which they were displayed on the previous page and click on Confirm.

12. Once you have correctly entered your phrase in the MetaMask wallet, the wallet is ready to use. You will immediately be able to add your tokens to the wallet by uploading them from centralized trading sites such as Bitstamp, for instance. Click on All Done.

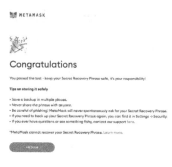

HOW TO BUY CRYPTOCURRENCIES ON BITSTAMP?

1. Log into your Bitstamp account.
2. Go to the Markets tab.

3. Find the cryptocurrency you wish to buy, such as USDC or ETH. Click on the Trade button.
4. In the top right corner of the screen, select the currency you have deposited into your account from your bank (USD, EUR, GBP...) next

proceed to Find Assets and to the icon that opens your profile.

5. Below that, select the amount of selected currency you want to buy. I entered 1000 USDC and the system warned me that I didn't have the funds to do so. Provided that you have previously deposited funds on Bitstamp, you will not have this problem and the following two steps will be completed without any problems.

6. The system will recalculate automatically the amount of the selected cryptocurrency you will receive.

7. Click on the Buy button, confirm the transaction and the chosen cryptocurrency will immediately appear in your account.

HOW TO TRANSFER CRYPTOCURRENCIES FROM BITSTAMP TO METAMASK?

1. On the top bar click on Withdrawal and then Cryptocurrency.
2. From the list provided, select the cryptocurrency purchased and click Continue.

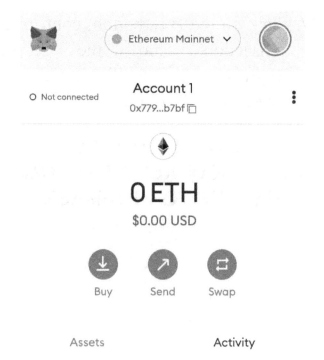

3. In the MetaMask wallet, click on Account 1... 0x... which will copy your wallet address to the clipboard.

4. Then paste the copied address of the MetaMask wallet on the Bitstamp exchange website under Destination Address.

5. In the Address Label you can optionally name your wallet so that

you do not have to paste it again in the future.

6. Enter the amount of cryptocurrency you wish to transfer and click on Authenticate & Withdraw button.

7. Confirm the operation at the end. The tokens will usually be in your MetaMask wallet after a few minutes or so.

HOW TO CONVERT USDC TO HEX?

Once you have successfully set up MetaMask, you need to buy Ethereum (ETH). Unless you have previously transferred it from Bitstamp or another exchange. You can also buy Ethereum by entering MetaMask using the deposit or buy function inside our wallet. In order to do so:

1. Click on Buy and then Continue to Wyre or another preferred service provider. For transactions over $1,000 you will have to undergo identity verification, similar to Bitstamp. In this case, it is better to use Bitstamp and transfer the funds to MetaMask.

2. When you get to the next screen, enter the amount in USD that you want to convert to ETH. You will then be shown the amount in ETH and the charged fee.

3. After accepting the amount, click I authorize... and Next.

4. In the next window, complete your details and insert your card number.

5. Click on Submit and ETH will appear in your wallet after a few minutes. With ETH or ETH and USDC or another cryptocurrency in your wallet, you can finally become the proud owner of HEX.

6. Go to HEX.com and on the right-hand side click on the Connect Wallet button. Select MetaMask and confirm the connection. Now your wallet works directly with the Uniswap exchange.

7. When you connect your wallet to the exchange, enter the ETH amount or other cryptocurrency amount you want to exchange for HEX. The system will automatically recalculate how much HEX you will receive.

8. If you have sufficient funds to perform the transaction, click on Swap and confirm the transaction. After the transaction, the HEX tokens will be added to your MetaMask wallet balance.

HOW TO BUY HEX ON SIMPLEX?

Simplex is a licensed financial institution, enabling its extensive network of partners to accept the widest range of payment methods, including: Visa, MasterCard, Apple Pay, SWIFT, SEPA and others. From August 2022, you can buy HEX there in a very straightforward manner:

1. Go to buy.hex.com. Enter the HEX amount you want to buy. Simplex will automatically show you how much it will cost you in your chosen currency. In the case above, I want to buy 10,000 HEX which will cost me €465.01. In the ERC-20 (HEX) address field, paste the address of your MetaMask wallet. In the MetaMask wallet, click on Account 1... 0x... which will copy your wallet

address to the clipboard. Then paste the copied MetaMask wallet address into the ERC-20 (HEX) address field on buy.simplex.com. Click on Continue button.

2. On the next page, enter the details of the credit card you wish to use to pay for the HEX purchase. You may, but do not have to, tick off the box Save card for my future purchases if you expect to use this method of purchasing HEX frequently. Tick I have read and agreed to the Terms and Conditions and Privacy Policy and click on Next. Follow the next

steps as instructed on the screen and your purchased HEX will soon be in your wallet.

HOW TO STAKE AND UNSTAKE HEX?

Staking (freezing) tokens to generate interest is entirely voluntary and optional. Alternatively, you can simply buy and hold HEX in your wallet without any further interaction under the HEX contract. Assuming the price of the token rises in the long term, you will one day be able to sell it at a higher price. While you wait, however, you will not accrue interest averaging between 10 and 40 per cent per year depending on the length of the stake. HEX staking is very simple:

1. Open MetaMask and go to go.hex.com/stake in your browser.
2. Click on the Connect button in the top right corner.

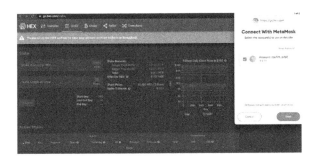

3. Allow to continue and the wallet will connect to go.hex.com/stake

4. Here you set the stake (the amount of
HEX to be placed in the long-term
deposit) and specify the term of your
investment. The deposit amount and
the term will affect the return on your
investment. The higher the amount,
the higher the opportunity to generate
profit. The minimum deposit period
is 1 day. The maximum deposit
period is 5555 days. Using the
Longer Pays Better HEX bonus, you
can get 3 times more shares for the
same amount of HEX. All you have
to do is choose a Stake Length longer
than 3.641 days.

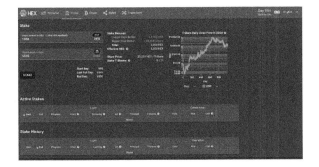

5. When choosing the term of your deposit, remember that you will not be able to terminate the deposit before maturity without a serious penalty, which could even consume your entire investment.

6. Once you selected the amount and duration of the deposit, click on Stake. Give consent in MetaMask and confirm the transaction.

7. HEX will disappear from your wallet in MetaMask as it will be temporarily burnt.

8. You can track the progress of your stake on go.hex.com/stake when it is linked to your MetaMask wallet or via the staker.app.

9. When your stake matures after the investment term you have decided on, then you will have to finish it.
10. To do this, on go.hex.com/stake after connecting to the MetaMask wallet, use the End Stake option.

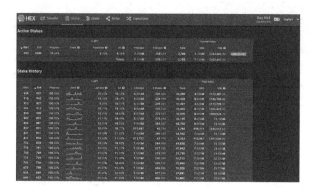

11. Make sure the button is in black. It means that you can end your stake. If the End Stake button is in red, you are trying to end it too early and you will be financially penalized. At best, you will lose some or all of your accrued interest and at worst some or all of your investment. For your own

good, do not end your stakes early, no matter what!

HOW TO BUY PULSECHAIN AND PULSEX?

When I am writing these words PulseChain and PulseX have not yet been launched. I am therefore unable to describe in detail the process of purchasing PLS and PLSX tokens. However, the process will be very similar to the one I described in the section How to convert USDC to HEX?. The website www.hex.com will offer an option to link the MetaMask wallet directly to the PulseX exchange, just as it is currently linked to the Uniswap exchange.

Below I will show you how to buy PLS and PLSX using ETH and other tokens in the Ethereum network in the test version of PulseChain. The operations illustrated above should look almost identical in the official version of PulseChain. I believe that if you have read this book this far, you will be able to work out any differences, if any, between the test and official versions of PulseChain and PulseX on your own.

You will first need to transfer funds from the Ethereum network to the PulseChain network. In order to do this:

1. Go to www.pulseramp.com and link your wallet.

2. It is the so-called bridge (Pulse Bridge) that supports the transfer of cryptocurrencies between the Ethereum and PulseChain networks.

3. To start using the bridge you must switch the network to PulseChain. In the test case above, click on PULSECHAIN TESTNET and make a few required confirmations in MetaMask.

4. The double arrow symbol in the middle or top right corner defines which way the funds will be sent (ETHaPulseChain   or

PulseChainaETH). Select the currency you intend to send, e.g. ETH, and enter how much you are sending, e.g. 0.7 ETH. Click Send. Check the transaction details on the next screen and if everything is correct press Send once again.

5. After approximately 30 seconds, you will receive transfer confirmation . Your sample 0.7 ETH, is now 0.6993 eETH (due to bridge fees) on the PulseChain network. The name eETH comes from the fact that ETH originally lives on the Ethereum network, not PulseChain. The›e points precisely to this network. So in essence you are using Wrapped Ethereum on PulseChain. The pPLS or pPLSX token suggests that these are tokens on the PulseChain network and so on.

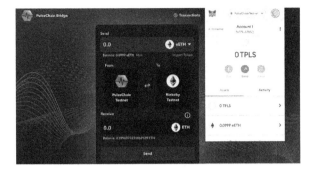

6. Click on the double arrow symbol to change the transfer direction.
7. Then click on Import token.
8. On the next screen, click Add token which will make the eETH visible in Assets in your MetaMask wallet.

The aforementioned process will look identical for other tokens, such as HEX, Chainlink, Shiba Inu or Wrapped Bitcoin.

With funds on the PulseChain network, we can start playing on the PulseX exchange.

1. In the MetaMask wallet under the Assets tab, click on the eETH token and then on the button representing the three dots in the top right corner.

2. Then click on Token details and copy the Token Contract Address to the clipboard.

3. Go to www.pulsex.com and link it to the MetaMask wallet.

4. Click on the first box in the Swap tab and then on Manage Tokens.

5. Select Tokens next to Lists. Paste the address copied to the clipboard in the appropriate field and click Import.

6. Now, in the SWAP tab, you can select an eETH token and convert it into PLSX, for instance. Select the amount of eETH you want to swap, e.g. 0.0999.

7. The system will automatically calculate how much PLSX you will get for this, e.g. 0.1 eETH = 31,709.7 PLSX.

8. Click Enable ETH and give all consents in MetaMask. Then click Swap and confirm the transaction. After a few moments, the your eETH

balance will be reduced by the selected amount and you will see the corresponding amount of PLSX in Assets in your MetaMask wallet.

The aforementioned process will look identical for other swaps, e.g. eETH to PLS or PLSX to HEX and vice versa. If you held ETH or Ethereum-based tokens such as HEX, PulseDoge or Tether (USDT) in MetaMask at PulseChain launch date, you will be able to freely swap them on www.pulsex.com without using Pulse Bridge.

WALLET ALLOCATION

The HEX value on the Ethereum network went up 10 000 times between January 2020 and September 2021. While I write these words (August 2022), its price is around 5 cents apiece with the forecast that in the next bull market the price will rise to a minimum of $4-5 and a maximum of $10-

25. So we are talking about an increase of between 100 and 500 times.

Richard Heart has mentioned on a number of occasions that he would like HEX to be expensive on both the Ethereum and the PulseChain networks.There are indications, therefore, that the price of HEX in the PulseChain network will also rise rapidly and it is possible that it will go head-to-head with the HEX price in the Ethereum network.

If the value of the 'weakest' of the new blockchains, such as Tron or Avax, for instance have gone up 'only' between 120 and 150 times within 1.5-4 year timeframe, it seems reasonable to assume that the far superior PulseChain will guarantee at least identical returns to early investors. It should also not be forgotten that the project most similar to PulseChain, Ethereum, has increased in value by almost 3,000 times. The prices of the decentralized exchange's tokens rose from 1000% (1Inch) to 5000% (SUSHI) in the first 130 days and between

20,000% (LRC) and 268,000% (Rune) in less than 700 days. The question about much better PulseX performance will be brought by the future.

Above you can see only the projections because I cannot accurately predict whether it is possible to make the greatest amount of money in the fastest way by investing in PulseChain, PulseX or perhaps in HEX on one or both blockchains. Having, let's say, $10,000 at my disposal, I would invest equally in eHEX, HEX, PLS and PLSX, buying tokens of each type for the equivalent of $2,500, and then wait patiently for the next bull market...

SUMMARY

- Your future wallet should consist of four products to start with: (e)HEX on the Ethereum blockchain, HEX on the PulseChain blockchain PLS – the native token of the PulseChain PLSX exchange.

- In the future, I would pay due attention to Richard Heart's next ventures, such as an unnamed incentive token for PulseX liquidity providers, crypto wallets (alternatives to MetaMask and others), direct collaboration solutions between traditional banks and PulseChain network-based products.

- Start investing in crypto by opening an account on Bitstamp, one of the largest, popular and easy-to-use cryptocurrency exchanges.

- There are many wallets for handling cryptocurrencies. One of the most popular and best wallets to handle Ethereum and PulseChain-based products is MetaMask. This should be your second step as a novice crypto investor.

- You can buy HEX by swapping USDC or ETH in your MetaMask wallet by connecting it to www.hex.com or by using www.buy.hex.com.

- Staking (freezing) tokens to generate interest is completely voluntary and optional. You can handle staking by connecting MetaMask to www.go.hex.com/stake.

- As I write these words PulseChain and PulseX have not yet been launched. I am therefore unable to describe in detail the process of purchasing PLS and PLSX tokens. However, the process will be very similar to that I described in the section How to convert USDC to HEX?.

- Detailed instructions for all the aforementioned steps can be found in the section above.

- We cannot accurately predict whether it is possible to make the greatest amount of money in the fastest way by investing in PulseChain, PulseX or perhaps in HEX on one or both blockchains. Having, let's say, $10,000 at my disposal, I would invest equally in eHEX, HEX, PLS and PLSX, buying tokens of each type for the equivalent of $2,500, and then wait patiently for the next bull market....

CHAPTER 9
SECURITY - HOW NOT TO LOSE ALL YOUR MONEY

I was breaking people, not passwords.

Kevin Mitnick – American computer security consultant, author and convicted hacker.

I wrote about the problems, fraud, hacking and corruption in the crypto business in

Chapter Three. This represents just the tip of the iceberg when it comes to the dangers that await cryptocurrency investors. In my more than five years of crypto investing, I have never lost funds due to any of the typical risks in the crypto business. In this chapter, I will explain what you can do to avoid losing all your money.

CENTRALIZED EXCHANGES

When investing in cryptocurrencies, you will not protect yourself from using centralized exchanges. So think of them as a necessary evil. The less you have to deal with them, the better. The shorter your funds are in their possession, the safer.

Crypto exchanges are targeted by hackers all the time and even the major players in the business such as Binance, Bitfinex and Coinbase, are not spared. Despite the fact that sometimes funds can be recovered or the exchange takes responsibility for the lost money, it is not guaranteed and the recovery process can take ages. The customers of the Mt.Gox exchange hacked in 2011 are still promised today that they will be able to recover at least some of their lost Bitcoins.

Very often, when there are high price fluctuations in the crypto market, due to investor panic or euphoria, for instance, there are problems logging on to the exchange or withdrawing funds, which can take up to several days. Any attempts to contact Customer Service during such hectic times are generally futile effort.

There are cases where exchanges block customers' funds for reasons that are not always clear, and it can cost a lot of time and require strong nerves to unblock them. Kraken exchange kept blocking several thousand dollars of a friend of mine for over six months. During this time, he often tried unsuccessfully to work with customer service to prove that he was not a drug smuggler or did not launder dirty money.

One day I transferred cryptocurrency worth €2,000 to the Binance exchange for the second time in my life with the plan to withdraw this amount to my bank account. After making the crypto transfer, it turned out that I was blocked from withdrawing funds to my bank. Customer service told me that transfers to/from the bank were blocked because my previous transactions were suspicious. However, due to Binance's company policy, I could not be told what was suspicious and how I could prove that I never did anything wrong. This will forever be a company secret. The problem could be solved indirectly by transferring cryptocurrency from Binance to another exchange, from which I managed to get the funds out to the bank.

Revolut Bank, where I have an account into which I was withdrawing funds from the Bitstamp exchange at one point also asked me to prove that I was not a criminal. It eventually accepted my documents but threatened to close my account if I continued to deposit funds into it from the Bitstamp exchange. Perhaps the reason for the whole situation was not suspicion of criminality but the fact that Revolut also has its own crypto trading platform, so Bitstamp is a competitor?

The exchanges I use, such as the current Bitstamp, Bitkub and Zonda (formerly Bitbay) regularly freeze my accounts, requesting re-verification of identity and tax residency information. Fortunately, so far this happens when I don't happen to have funds or transfers pending with them. However, taking into account the fact that I never know when the next verification awaits me, I always try to keep my funds, which are held by the exchange even for a short period, in small amounts. I prefer to make several or even over a dozen small transfers in a row, rather than a single large transfer that will be blocked for an unknown period of time.

Centralized exchanges often offer a whole array of other services, such as crypto wallets to hold funds, staking platforms or savings accounts and much more. Taking into account all I described above, I have never used these types of services. I do not intend to do so and I recommend you to stay away from them too. By using exchanges and the products they offer, the exchange, not you, is in possession of your private key which is the equivalent of your bank account PIN. Stick to the principle of not your keys, not your crypto.

If I have not convinced you yet, make sure you carefully read the terms and conditions of the exchange you are using. Many, if not all, of them have, among other things, a statement there that they reserve the right to retain your funds forever without giving reason thereof or to use them for various purposes in the event of bankruptcy or other problems with their platform.

NOT YOUR KEYS, NOT YOUR CRYPTO

As you begin your adventure with cryptocurrencies, you will encounter the concepts of public keys and private keys. Understanding the difference between them and how to use them is incredibly important for the security of your investments.

The public key is used to send cryptocurrency to the wallet. The private key is used to verify the transaction and confirm ownership of the Blockchain address. If someone sends you, let's say, 1000 HEX, the private key will be required to unlock that transaction and prove that you now own 1000 HEX. Think of your public key as your bank account number. You can share it with whomever you wish, who can then send money there. However, knowing your bank account number does not allow anyone to withdraw money or otherwise log in your account. An example of the public key format is:

0x9525395b11aF3f57668A342bDa0E31c 84dE13cDc.

The private key is the most important password for your crypto wallet. It acts like the PIN to your bank account or the password to your email address. Only you should have access to it and keep it secret. You need to understand that if someone knows your private key, he or she will have access to all the cryptocurrencies in that wallet and can do whatever he or she want with it. The function of the private key, technically speaking, is to sign transactions that use your funds. Transactions using your funds cannot be verified by the network without the private key attached. The public key encrypts transactions that can only be decrypted with the corresponding private key.

Private keys are numerical codes that look like that one below, for instance:

ea1f293fc442f43d912360ac73aadf4ca8a6 09d8a7693d8c4331f15cc9953cb8.

In order to make things more user-friendly, many wallet providers often encode the private key in a way that can be more easily saved and remembered.

Many wallets use an initial phrase, also known as a secret recovery phrase, to unlock the wallet. If you open a MetaMask crypto wallet, you are given a string of random words that you use to unlock your funds. Your private key is hidden in the software behind this user-friendly string of words. You must securely store and never share this particular string of words with anyone.

If you hold your crypto in an exchange wallet (such as Coinbase or Binance, for instance) or with a custodian, this company holds your private key for you. Strictly speaking, it controls your funds on your behalf and can do whatever it wants with it at any time. Hence the origin of the saying **not your keys, not your crypto.** Remember it once and for all and take it to your heart!

You must keep your private key safe and secret. Write it down and keep it in several places because, unlike bank PINs, there is no way of recovering it. If you lose your private key or it falls into the wrong hands, you can forget about the money in there.

The level of security for your private key depends on the size of your investment and, over time, probably progressing paranoia. It is a good idea to divide your private key regardless of how it is stored into two parts and keep them at different places. If someone finds one part, he or she is less likely to find the other. A sealed envelope among your other documents, steel plates such as Cryptotag Zeus or The Billfodl, to avoid destruction of your private key in the event of a flood or fire, kept in a safe deposit or bank box are also not bad ideas. And if you think that keeping a steel plate with your private key in a safe box is too obvious, you could always sink it into the bottom of the tomato soup you keep in the freezer...

Do not take screenshots or photos with your phone and do not save your private key in any file, as these digital copies are often the target of hackers.

SCAMMERS AND HACKERS

Scammers of all kinds will constantly try to get their hands on your private keys. You will receive emails and messages on all sorts of instant messengers telling you that you need to verify your wallet, your stock market account or that your funds are at risk and you now need to go to a certain website and enter your private key.

My email was on a list of addresses that leaked to the Web from Ledger company, one of the manufacturers of crypto wallets. Since I am a customer of Ledger, it is obvious that I own a certain amount of crypto. Since then, I have regularly received emails from various suspicious people and organizations. One of them informed me that my wallet on the Binance exchange was blocked and it required KYC (Know Your Customer) re-verification. I didn't have a wallet on Binance. I haven't used the exchange's services for a long time either. However, the email looked very realistic and it scared me of the consequences. I do not know where the Verify Now button at the bottom of the email led to because I have never clicked it. I assume that the scam system will ask for my Binance exchange login and password, private keys or install suspicious software on my computer.

Ask a question about MetaMask on Twitter, for instance, and the scammer bots will immediately generate comments with links to pages that will help you as long as you enter your private key there. Ask for help with anything on the official HEX.COM channel on Telegram and you will quickly find that one of the tens of thousands of participants on that channel is a scammer who will send you a private message claiming to be an official HEX customer service agent. For this reason, Richard Heart and many other influencers in the crypto business entered in their descriptions the information that they would never send you a private message first.

Examples are abundant and could be listed endlessly, but I think it should be clear at this stage that dangers lurk behind every corner and you should not trust anyone.

YOUR CRYPTO WALLET

Hopefully, at this stage you are already convinced that all exchanges and other intermediaries are a necessary evil and that you need to equip yourself with your own crypto wallet. One of the simplest, best and safest solutions is the wallet offered by www.metamask.io. In Chapter 8 I have described in detail how to you can set up your own wallet. Remember to go directly to the website I specified rather than typing the words MetaMask into Google because the list of results you get can take you to a fake MetaMask website with a fake wallet. When setting up a wallet at www.metamask.io, remember to save, securely store and not share your private keys with anyone:-).

The MetaMask wallet is completely sufficient for you if your planned investment or funds held there do not exceed $1,000. If you plan to hold more than $10,000 of crypto, you should purchase the so-called hardware wallet. Remember that even a small investment of $1,000 can easily grow to $10,000. The most popular, but not the only hardware wallets, are offered by www.ledger.com and www.trezor.io.

The main difference between software-based wallets such as MetaMask and hardware-based wallets such as Ledger or Trezor is that in the latter case you will need a physical device to verify each transaction. It is therefore impossible to hack your wallet via Web without physical access to your Ledger or Trezor.

Order one of these and when you receive it, follow the instructions to perform setup, which is very straightforward . As with MetaMask, both Ledger and Trezor will generate new private keys for you. Proceed with them in exactly the same manner as I described in the previous section. When ordering one of these wallets, make sure you buy them directly from the manufacturers at www.ledger.com or www.trezor.io. Any other physical or online shop like Amazon is a risk that your private key has already been generated and copied by an unauthorized person. If your crypto investment exceeds $1 million, then consider a multi-sig setup with www.gnosis-safe.io. In general, multi-sig requires multiple wallets to be signed before a transaction can take place. This is a little more complicated than using a hardware wallet, but well worth the effort for larger cryptocurrency investments. This is especially true for long-term deposits, such as staking HEX for 5555 days. As an alternative to Gnosis Safe, you could spread your cryptocurrencies across several wallets like Ledger or Trezor.

LAPTOPS AND SMARTPHONES

When I introduce someone to the world of crypto and mention MetaMask for the first time, often the person will reach for his or her phone to download a wallet onto it. As a general rule, I advise against using wallets or performing any crypto transactions on a smartphone because it is less secure than using a laptop or desktop computer.... Smartphones are easier to hack, steal and lose. Personally, I don't have a single wallet on my phone and I don't carry out any transactions via my mobile. This rule also applies to the use of exchanges and I highly recommend following it.

When using a computer, you should also follow a few basic security rules. Whether you are using an operating system Microsoft Windows or Mac OS, you should use anti-virus software, a firewall and a VPN as a bare minimum. The next step for increasing your security should be to have a separate personal computer dedicated solely to working with cryptocurrencies. Such a computer should be equipped with the minimum and necessary software to function as well as a web browser, antivirus, firewall and VPN. This computer should only be connected to the Web when you intend to perform any transaction and disconnected once it has been finalized. If the aforementioned requirements sound to you like too much expense or a process requiring too much hassle, ask yourself if you are really right when you may own or soon will own crypto worth tens to hundreds of thousands of dollars, if not even millions.

LACK OF CUSTOMER SERVICE

Despite numerous avoidable risks lurking behind every corner , it is often the case that you are your own worst enemy. The nature of the blockchain technology on which the cryptocurrency system is based means that all transactions are irreversible. If, when sending money between banks, you make a mistake in the recipient's account number, that cash will most likely come back to you with or without the intervention of the bank's customer service department.

When sending cryptocurrencies, there are no intermediaries (customer service) to help you if, for instance, you misspell the recipient's wallet address. If you accidentally send money to me and not to your brother, and we are friends, there is no problem. I will send the money back to you after receiving a message from you about it. However, if you send crypto to an address whose owner you do not know because you accidentally typed f' instead of e, you will never get it back because you will not know where your money is now and who you should contact.

Wallets, exchanges and other cryptocurrency service providers have already done a lot to eliminate as many of these potential situations as possible anyway. Complicated wallet addresses can be copied to the clipboard with a single click, ensuring that no one in their right mind would type them in manually. This option makes it impossible to copy an address with a missing number or letter at its beginning or end. If you use this option, you should still check carefully whether the address you copied is really the one you want to send money to. Fraudsters long time ago have developed software that can install itself on your computer without your knowledge and replace the pasted address directly on the clipboard! If you have copied an address from the exchange and are sending funds from your wallet and if you do not check that the address pasted in your wallet is exactly the same as the one you have just copied from the exchange, you can end up sending funds directly to the fraudster.

When operating in the cryptocurrency market, you need to understand that all responsibility is in your hands and if you make such fundamental mistakes, you only have yourself to blame and no one will be able to help you. However, this is a small price to pay for an opportunity to turn relatively small amounts of money into millions.

SAFETY IN THE REAL WORLD

Wesley Passano, a 19-year-old crypto investor, bragged about his wealth and inspiring lifestyle on Instagram to his 133,000 followers and on Youtube to his 15,600 subscribers. In one photo, he stands leaning against his red Porsche, holding a thick bundle of banknotes. In August 2021, he was driving to his barbershop in the Brazilian city of Sao Pedro de Aldeia when unknown perpetrators opened fire on him in broad daylight in front of multiple witnesses. Wesley died on the spot and his passenger was injured. The shocking killing was the work of gangs increasingly targeting bragging crypto traders and influencers after they flaunted their wealth on social media.

Kieren Hamilton, another crypto investor who is 21 years old and highly popular on social media, was attacked by two masked robbers who broke into his house home in Greater Manchester, Great Britain, and demanded valuables. He was stabbed in the arm before the robbers fled with his dog, worth approx. £1,000, an Apple MacBook laptop, gold bracelets and a gold wedding ring. Mr Hamilton's baby daughter was at home screaming in her cot when the robbers attacked at 6 a.m. on 5 January 2018.

Tjeerd H., a 39-year-old crypto trader, was robbed and tortured at his home in Drouwenerveen, the Netherlands, in 2019. The perpetrators disguised as police from a special SWAT team tied him up, hanged him, waterboarded him, beat him and drilled seven holes in his leg with an impact drill.

The above examples are just an illustration of what can happen when you become financially successful in crypto business and do not also take care of your security in the real world.

Richard Heart moved out of the USA 15 years ago and almost never returns there because he believes the country is far more dangerous for supposed multi-billionaires like him. Richard lives somewhere in Europe, although no one apart from his family and closest friends knows where. When meeting fans of his products in various European cities, he announced the exact time and location of the meeting several hours before it was actually held, so as not to give potential villains too much time to prepare a potential attack.

Many cryptocurrency investors do not use social media at all or hardly at all. Others use pseudonyms or do not publish photos or videos of themselves at all. Still others do not publish anything to do with crypto, money or the luxurious life they lead. There are many methods to avoid becoming a target: from remaining as anonymous as possible through learning martial arts and owning weapons, to hiring private security guards and buying guard dogs. Much depends on the country you live in and the laws, lifestyle and individual preferences there. One thing is for sure though, the examples given above of what can happen if you don't exercise caution after being successful with cryptocurrencies should make you treat your safety seriously.

SUMMARY

- When investing in cryptocurrencies, you will not avoid using centralized exchanges. So think of them as a necessary evil. The less you have to deal with them, the better.

- **Not your keys, not your crypto**

- The public key is used to send cryptocurrency to the wallet. The private key is used to verify transactions and confirm ownership of the Blockchain address.

- The private key is the most important password for your crypto wallet. It acts like the PIN to your bank account or the password to your email address. Only you should have access to it and keep it secret.

- It is a good idea to divide your private key, regardless of how it is stored, into two parts and keep them at different places. If someone finds one part, they are less likely to find the other.

- Do not take screenshots or photos with your phone and do not save your private key in any file because these digital copies are often the target of hackers.

- Scammers of all kinds will constantly try to get their hands on your private keys. You will receive emails and messages on all sorts of instant messengers telling you that you need to verify your wallet, your exchange account or that your funds are at risk and you now need to go to a certain website and enter your private key.

- One of the most straightforward, best and safest solutions is the wallet offered by www.metamask.io.

- If you plan to deposit more than $10,000 of cryptocurrency, you should purchase the so-called hardware wallet.

- The most popular, but not the only hardware wallets are offered by www.ledger.com and www.trezor.io.

- If your crypto investment exceeds $1 million, then consider a multi-sig setup with www.gnosis-safe.io. Essentially, multi-sig requires multiple wallets to be signed before a transaction can take place.

- Generally speaking, I would advise against using wallets or performing any crypto transactions on a smartphone because it is less secure than using a laptop or desktop computer.

- When using a personal computer, you should also follow a few basic security rules. Whether you using Microsoft Windows or Mac OS operating system, you should use anti-virus software, a firewall and a VPN as a bare minimum.

- The next step to enhance your security should be to have a separate computer dedicated solely to working with cryptocurrencies.

- Despite numerous avoidable risks lurking behind every corner, it is often the case that you are your own worst enemy. The nature of the blockchain technology on which the cryptocurrency system is based means that all transactions are irreversible. When sending cryptocurrencies, there are no intermediaries (customer service) to help you if, for instance, you misspell the recipient's wallet address.

- Take safety precautions in the real world.
- Many cryptocurrency investors do not use social media at all or hardly at all. Others use pseudonyms or do not publish photos or videos of themselves at all. Still others do not publish anything to do with crypto, money or the luxurious life they lead.
- There are numerous methods to avoid becoming a target of attackers: from remaining as anonymous as possible, learning martial arts and owning weapons, to hiring private security guards and buying guard dogs.

CHAPTER 10
TAX OPTIMIZATION

*Taxation is theft, purely and simply
even though it is theft on a grand
and colossal scale which no
acknowledged criminals could hope
to match. It is a compulsory seizure
of the property of the State's
inhabitants, or subjects.*

Murray N. Rothbard

The growing popularity of cryptocurrencies has caused tax offices in many countries to take an interest in the topic.

Cryptocurrency in the USA is treated like real estate and other investments, not currencies. If you hold your cryptocurrency for a minimum of one year after purchase, you can qualify for a rate of 0 to 20% depending on your income. Shorter investments and trading are taxed at the levels between 10 and 37%.

In the UK, natural persons pay capital gains tax on their total gains above the annual tax-free allowance of £12,300. Any gains above this allowance will be taxed at 10% up to the basic tax rate (if available) and 20% on gains at higher and additional tax rates.

The success you may enjoy while investing into cryptocurrencies may make you start to consider moving to another country or at least changing or obtaining additional tax residency. Here are some ideas:

PORTUGAL

Portugal was one of the best places in the world to live if you wanted to avoid paying taxes on cryptocurrencies. Cryptocurrency trading was not considered to be investment income, so it was tax-free.

That was provided that you were not running a cryptocurrency company, your digital investments were also exempt from VAT and income tax in Portugal. For the vast majority of investors, Portugal was therefore a tax-free country for cryptocurrencies. Changes are coming next year. Profits made on digital-asset holdings held for less than one year will be taxed at a rate of 28%, while crypto held longer than that will be exempt from taxes, according to the country's 2023 budget plan. Authorities will also treat gains from the issuance of cryptocurrencies and mining operations as taxable income. The new policy will effectively end Portugal's status as a crypto tax haven in Europe. Portugal still has most of the things crypto investors and startups need to flourish: an aspiring tech scene, affordable living costs, great internet connectivity and even a visa for digital nomads. Add in about 300 days of sunshine per year, plenty of surf and tax breaks for foreign residents.

PUERTO RICO

American residents have probably heard of Silicon Valley billionaires heading south to enjoy the luxurious Puerto Rican lifestyle and enjoy the relaxed tax laws. Although Puerto Rico is an unincorporated territory of the United States, it is considered a foreign country in terms of federal income taxes. The country therefore sets its own tax laws.

When it comes to taxes on cryptocurrencies, this is great news. The residents of Puerto Rico pay a significantly lower territorial income tax compared to the US federal income tax rate. What's more, cryptocurrencies purchased while in Puerto Rico are completely exempt from capital gains tax, so whether you pay tax depends on when you bought your crypto. If you are an American resident who purchased cryptocurrency before moving to Puerto Rico, you still need to comply with IRS tax rules on cryptocurrencies. However, if you acquired your cryptocurrency after establishing residency in Puerto Rico, then it is completely exempt from capital gains tax.

SINGAPORE

There is a reason why many cryptocurrency exchanges, such as KuCoin and Phemex, are based in Singapore. Singapore is a tax haven for cryptocurrencies, both for natural persons and companies. This is because there is no capital gains tax in Singapore, so individual investors and companies are not required to pay cryptocurrency tax.

Furthermore, because cryptocurrencies are seen as intangible property from a tax perspective, when you spend cryptocurrencies on goods and services, it is seen as barter rather than payment. As a result, while goods or services can be subject to value-added tax, a coin or payment token, is no longer subject to this tax.

Of course, it is not possible to avoid all taxes. If you operate as a business and accept cryptocurrencies as payment, you will pay income tax on them. Similarly, if the company's core service is related to cryptocurrency trading, the company will still be liable for income tax.

Other crypto-friendly countries include: Germany, Belarus (!), El Salvador, Malaysia, Malta, the Cayman Islands, Switzerland, Georgia and the United Arab Emirates.

***

The greater the value of your cryptocurrency wallet, the potentially greater the tax problems but also the greater the opportunities to solve them. As a general rule of thumb, the less developed and the more foreign investment-hungry country, the easier it is to avoid or minimize taxes.

Many of these countries are also very pleasant places to live. Thailand, for instance, regularly changes its mind on crypto taxes, once mentioning a 20% tax and another time saying there will be no taxes at all by the end of 2023. All this changes little, given that more than half of Thais do not even have a Tax Identification Number. So who would care about a foreigner on a long-term tourist, marriage or business visa?

If you are not a citizen of the European Union but would like to be able to live there legally, many countries offer a special type of visa. For example, if you invest between €280,000 and €500,000 in Portugal, you can apply for the so-called Golden Visa which can be valid for a maximum of five years. At the end of this period, you qualify for Portuguese citizenship.

By investing in the Caribbean, you can obtain citizenship of Grenada, Antigua and Barbuda, Dominica, St Kitts and Nevis, St Lucia and others. The required level of investment starts from as little as $100,000.

For less than $50,000 you can become a tax resident of Paraguay where there is no tax on income generated from investments outside the country. After three years of being a resident, you can apply for a Paraguayan passport without necessarily living there all the time. Being a resident of the country allows you to live in Paraguay, Argentina, Brazil, Chile and Uruguay.

With another country's tax residency or passport, you can open bank accounts with the reassurance that your home country's tax authorities will not pursue you. Acting within the crypto-investor community, I have met tax residents of Uruguay with bank accounts in the Caribbean and living in Indonesia. Many of them also have multiple tax residences and several passports. As you can see, the options available are only limited by your needs, your imagination and the amount of money you have.

Tax evasion is of course a criminal offence mentioned in numerous, if not all legal codes. However, this does not change the fact that the so-called Panama Papers scandal a few years ago disclosed that at least five heads of state and many government officials, their families, friends and associates from more than 40 countries were using similar arrangements to optimize their taxes.

Dozens of celebrities such as Bono, Nicolas Cage and Pamela Anderson have also tried to evade tax payment and have suffered different consequences. Many of the 26 billionaires, including Elon Musk and Jeff Bezos, have paid only a fraction of the taxes compared to the average American. Although, this is because their income comes from various investments rather than a salary like in the case of the most of us. Could it be that tax optimization is only illegal or unethical when it affects us average and ordinary citizens?

SUMMARY

- 'Taxation is theft, purely and simply even though it is theft on a grand and colossal scale which no acknowledged criminals could hope to match. It is a compulsory seizure of the property of the State's inhabitants, or subjects.' – Murray N. Rothbard

- Several crypto investor-friendly jurisdictions include Portugal, Puerto Rico, Singapore, Germany, Belarus (!), El Salvador, Malaysia, Malta, the Cayman Islands, Switzerland, Georgia and the United Arab Emirates.

- As a general rule of thumb, the less developed and the more foreign investment-hungry country, the easier it is to avoid tax payment or to minimize them.

- If you are not a citizen of the European Union but would like to be able to live there legally, many countries offer a special type of visa. For example, if you invest between €280,000 and €500,000 in Portugal, you can apply for the so-called Golden Visa, which can be valid for a maximum of five years.

- By investing in the Caribbean, you can obtain citizenship of Grenada, Antigua and Barbuda, Dominica, St. Kitts and Nevis, St. Lucia and others. The required level of investment starts from as little as $100,000.

- For less than $50,000 you can become a tax resident of Paraguay, where there is no tax on income generated by investments made outside the country.

- Tax evasion is of course a criminal offence mentioned in numerous, if not all, legal codes.

- However, this does not change the fact that the so-called 'Panama Papers' scandal a few years ago revealed that at least five heads of state and many government officials, their families, friends and associates from more than 40 countries were using similar arrangements to optimize their taxes.

CONCLUSION

I've never been a full-time employee person. Taking into account over a dozen of bosses I encountered in my 20+ year long career, I liked only one. Although at that time I did not appreciate how lucky I was. I was always pissed off by the corporate politics and by the fact that at many of workplaces, it was more important to brown-nose rather than to present the qualifications and enthusiasm for the job, which I never lacked.

When I started my adventure with cryptocurrencies in 2017, I never thought that in just a few years they would allow me to achieve what I have dreamed of all my adult life. The beginnings were not easy. I did not know how it all worked. I made a lot of mistakes. I did not earn profits at the end of the bull market. I was holding paper losses for over two years. I mistakenly bought more cryptocurrencies in the middle of the bear market, thinking that prices would not fall again.

Finding HEX among tens of thousands of other cryptocurrency projects is a bit of coincidence and a bit of luck. After all, if it was not for my friend - Konrad, I may never have discovered Richard Heart and would have missed out on the Second Crypto Revolution. However, early investment in HEX, PulseChain and PulseX is already the result of thousands of hours spent on listening, watching and reading what their founder has to say. Moreover, these are also brave decisions on the verge of gambling and an inner conviction that I know what I am doing and that I must succeed this time.

I vividly remember, as if it was yesterday, when a good friend of mine in Mexico suggested me to sell everything when the value of my investments went up 5 times by mid-2020 and I was observing it in disbelief. Fortunately, I didn't listen to him and during Q1 of the following year my net worth rose by another 5 times in total multiplying the money I had invested in HEX by 25 times. I still sold almost nothing to multiply my money by another 50 times in the following quarter. About half of this amount was available for immediate sale because the rest was staked.

It was money I never dreamed of and which would allow me to provide for myself and my entire family for the rest of my life. However, I only took a few per cent of the profit and, from today's perspective, I know that it was far too little. Over the course of the next year, the value of my crypto-assets fell by 95 per cent at the worst time. I sat catatonic at home in Phuket in disbelief, watching HEX, which less than a year ago cost around $0.5, plunge to less than 3 cents.

Despite not selling my last top, I have not lost my relatively newly gained financial freedom and there is no indication that this is about to change in the nearest future.

However, new dreams of my own villa with a pool and a Lamborghini in the garage will have to wait for the bull market to return. I have no doubt that it will come again. Taking into account the size of my HEX wallet, the sacrifices on PulseChain and PulseX and assuming everything goes according to plan, I will come out much better off even under a conservative scenario than I could have done in September 2021.

If you got the impression that I was a hopeless fan boy of Richard Heart and his products, you were right. Now at least you know why. The founder of HEX sees no reason why HEX should not increase another 10,000 times from about 5 cents per 1 HEX. The more conservative forecasts of other people in the ecosystem assume multiples of 100-1000x. Richard does not speculate on the price of PulseChain and PulseX. Although taking into account how similar these products behaved in the past, anything between a multiple of at least 500 and 3000x is within reach. Any invested $1,000 could therefore turn into a minimum of $100,000-500,000. The maximum prices are not known to anyone and the market will decide on them.

Are you ready for a Second Crypto Revolution?

CPSIA information can be obtained
at www.ICGtesting.com
Printed in the USA
LVHW080848140723
752124LV00002B/91

9 781806 306961